D0786708

Springer Series on Social Work
Albert R. Roberts, D.S.W., Series Editor
Graduate School of Social Work, Rutgers, The State University of New Jersey

Advisory Board: Joseph D. Anderson, D.S.W., Barbara Berkman, D.S.W., Paul H. Ephross, Ph.D., Sheldon R. Gelman, Ph.D., Paul H. Glasser, Ph.D., and Julia Watkins, Ph.D.

Michael J. Smith, D.S.W., is a professor at the Hunter College School of Social Work in New York City. He is a member of the Masters Program Faculty at Hunter College. He is also on the Faculty of the Doctoral Program in Social Welfare at the City University of New York. He was Senior Research Consultant at the Community Service Society of New York and a member of the Research Department of the Child Welfare League of America. Professor Smith is the author of numerous articles on family support programs, single-parent families, developmentally disabled children, child welfare programs, and social movements. He is the co-author of a book on family care of the elderly.

Program Evaluation in the Human Services

Michael J. Smith, D.S.W.

Foreword by Harold Lewis

SPRINGER PUBLISHING COMPANY
New York

Springer Publishing Company, Inc.
536 Broadway
New York, NY 10012

90 91 92 93 94 / 5 4 3 2 1

Library of Congress Cataloging-in-Publication Data

Smith, Michael J.
    Program evaluation in the human services / Michael J. Smith;
foreword by Harold Lewis.
        p.   cm—(Springer series on social work; v. 16)
    Includes bibliographic references.
    ISBN 0-8261-6590-7
    1. Human services—Evaluation.   I. Title.   II. Series.
HV40.S615, 1990
316.3'068—dc20

Printed in the United States of America

Contents

Foreword

Introducing a learner to a complex subject through a simplified presentation of its essentials is a demanding task. The sophisticate more often prefers to engage his or her peers in discussions of the cutting edge issues of their discipline, assuming the necessary understanding that such discussion requires. It is therefore a rare occurrence to read an introductory text written by an accomplished practitioner in which the essentials are identified and addressed and the temptations to pursue the subject in depth appropriately avoided.

That Professor Smith, an accomplished scholar of the practice of evaluative research in the human services, has taken the time to write such an introductory text is commendable. As the reader will note, simplification necessitates demystification, illustration and repetition, and calls for a sound grasp of fundamentals. The resulting product is enlightening to the sophisticate as well as the novice. Professor Smith's peers, as well as their pupils, can benefit from this volume, particularly in the respect and concern it evidences for the subject addressed, and the students for whom it is intended.

HAROLD LEWIS, Dean
Hunter College School of Social Work
New York, New York

Acknowledgments

I would like to express my appreciation to Harold Lewis, Dean of the Hunter College School of Social Work for his suggestions and comments on an early draft of the manuscript. I also want to thank Francis G. Caro, Professor and Director of Research, Gerontological Institute, University of Massachusetts at Boston, for reading an early draft and sharing his views on program evaluation.

Professor Albert R. Roberts of the Rutgers University School of Social Work, the series editor, recognized the potential of my idea at an early point. Barbara Watkins, Kathleen O'Malley, and Pamela Lankas of Springer Publishing helped with the final product. I hope the product meets everyone's expectations.

My wife, Rosemarie Rerisi Smith, has provided me with nothing but support, encouragement, and organization ever since I have known her. Elizabeth Erin Smith and Suzanne Meghan Smith are special daughters who make our family life happy and interesting.

MICHAEL J. SMITH, D.S.W.
Hunter College
New York, New York

Program Evaluation in the
Human Serivces

1 An Introduction to Program Evaluation

This book will provide students and professionals in social work and the human services with an introduction on how to evaluate human service programs. Human service programs are programs designed to help people in settings such as social service agencies, mental health clinics, health settings, child welfare agencies, family counseling agencies, counseling programs in schools, and in numerous other settings.

How can program evaluation help you? Program evaluation can help human service professionals assess a wide range of social programs. For example, is a group program for the parents of emotionally disturbed adolescents helping them understand the needs of their children better? Is a counseling program for employees helping them cope with their personal and family responsibilities? Are home care and counseling services improving the condition of families at risk of placing their children in foster care? As a social worker, or a human service practitioner supervisor, or an administrator, or as a caring professional these questions are important for you to ask. Consider the following situations, which you might encounter as a human service professional.

WHEN YOU NEED TO KNOW THE TECHNIQUES OF PROGRAM EVALUATION

A major urban hospital has an inpatient psychiatric treatment program for a chronic schizophrenic population. The program is supported by federal Medicaid funds, private medical insurance, and private fee for service payments. The average hospital stay is approximately three months. During that time patients are given intensive psychiatric treatment, prescribed medication, and supportive individual and group counseling from social workers and group programs that teach job-development skills. Hospital administrators ask the psychiatrists, social workers, and employment and recreational counselors if the program works. You are on the clinical staff of the hospital. You and your colleagues know of a few success stories in which the patients made very successful adjustments to the community, but lack time or resources to determine how the average person adjusts to the community after discharge from the hospital. Your supervisor asks you to help her answer some of the hospital administrators' concerns about the program. Where to you start? How can you help?

In a large high school in an upper middle-class neighborhood three students commit suicide in one year. The whole community is alarmed. Their stories fill the local and regional news media. No one knows why so many suicides occurred in such a short period of time. What are the causes? Drugs? Problems of adolescent self-image? Pressure in school? Concern about getting into the right college? The local Board of Education appropriates $200,000 for a suicide prevention counseling program. Five percent of the budget, or $10,000, is allocated to evaluate whether the program is helping the community with its problem. You are a student counselor at the high school and are chosen to head the program. This is an excellent career move for you. You also are responsible for seeing that the program gets evaluated. You know how to implement a counseling program, but what do you do about evaluating the program?

The president of a large university wants to establish a program that helps all university employees with their personal and family problems. The program assures confidentiality in that records from the program can never be used against employees who have problems. The program has been in existence for two years and over 200 employees have used the service. The program is used for problems ranging from caring for an elderly relative to counseling for married couples or for substance abuse. The president now wants to determine whether employees who came for service valued the program and what kind of a change it made in their lives. You are a counselor in the program and the program director wants you to determine the possible value of the program for those who used it. Where do you start?

A major drug treatment program that employs over 150 social workers and psychologists serves over 2,000 intravenous drug users each year. Estimates suggest that over 50 percent of the current client population is infected by the AIDS virus. Because of the debilitating effects of the disease, this group of clients seems to be drawing over 90 percent of the agency's direct service resources. Staff are concerned about this situation. They are overwhelmed by work and want to know the most efficient way to serve the group infected with the AIDS virus. You are hired to develop a training program for staff to increase their knowledge and skill in serving AIDS patients. As part of your responsibilities, administrators and staff want you to document the effects of the program you develop. How do you proceed?

Program evaluation and the techniques of program evaluation help us answer critical questions about human service programs. Is the program effective? Does it seem to be having the desired effect? Is the program on the right track? Are people benefitting? Are they accepting the service? Did they go to the social service agency to which you referred them? What was the outcome of the counseling they received? These are just a few of the questions program evaluation can help us answer.

Program evaluation also helps you formulate and reformulate the questions you should be asking with more precision. This book will introduce you to the basic techniques of program evaluation, which can be used to assess both the operations and outcomes of programs.

Surely you have wondered about the effectiveness of the counseling or social work *you* are delivering. You also have thought about whether the whole program works. Is this program successful, or at least, is it on the right track? The more you develop in your career, the more you also will want to answer these questions as someone involved in planning and administering social programs. Program evaluation can give us this essential, broader perspective on what we are doing.

Program evaluation is simply the application of a research methodology that will help you refine the kinds of questions you ask and help you answer questions about the operations and impact of social programs.

QUESTIONS ANSWERED THROUGH PROGRAM EVALUATION

Social programs are planned and implemented to achieve certain outcomes. The questions program evaluation answers are different depending on what you want to assess. You may have questions about the design or plan of the program—you want to assess the program plan. You may have questions about how the program works or is being implemented—you want to monitor program operations. You may want to look at the program's level of success or usefulness—you want to assess the program's outcome.

When you have program design or planning questions, you want to know: Is there a need for the program? Is there a program design? What is the program design? Is the intervention planned appropriate for the people served and the results desired? Is there any documentation in the literature that the program can be implemented? Does the program achieve the desired results?

When you want to assess how the program is being implemented, you want to know: Is the program serving anyone? How many people are being served? Is the program being implemented according to the program plan? What are the program's initial successes and failures? What are the major bottlenecks in implementing the program? Which of these are practical problems that can be overcome? Which problems point to major flaws in the program design? What are the initial costs of the program? Do the initial costs seem realistic?

When you want to assess the program's usefulness in achieving certain results, you want to know: What is the impact of the program? Which program goals are achieved? Which program goals are not achieved? Is the program efficient in achieving certain goals? Are the program costs too high given the level of impact? Are the program results clearly related to the program's impact?

As a technology, program evaluation is traditionally used to answer this wide range of questions on an aggregate or program level. The techniques of program evaluation are more typically and traditionally applied at this broader level to determine if programs achieve their goals, and if they benefit people.

For example, as a student in a Master's program in a school of social work, I worked in a program that served people recently released from prison. Since these men often did not have jobs upon their release, they needed money to get on their feet and until they obtained employment. The agency had a referral service whereby short-term financial assistance was made available for immediate needs. The person also was referred to the local welfare office to seek more substantial financial assistance until he could locate a job. Service loads were high, and it was often difficult to find out—when I referred people to welfare—whether or not they actually went to the welfare office. An even more important question was: Did they receive financial assistance from welfare?

More information was needed to see whether this program worked. The agency could have used program evaluation techniques to determine whether this part of the program was successful. On a personal level, I was continually frustrated in my concerns about how well this procedure worked, especially when we know of the reluctance of people to apply for welfare and the inaccessibility of the system.

Program evaluation techniques could have determined whether the referral procedure was successful. An evaluative study of that referral service could have provided information about any changes needed. An evaluative study also could have erased some of my personal concerns about the effectiveness of the referral procedures.

Program evaluation is essential in providing professional human service workers with this broader perspective on their practice. How many times are you involved in programs where you are uncertain that a service is useful? How many times are you involved in programs you suspect are successful, but which no one takes the time to document? Program evaluation can help provide documentation of the program's level of success or failure.

APPLYING PROGRAM EVALUATION TECHNIQUES TO YOUR PRACTICE

Program evaluation techniques also can be applied on a smaller scale to help you answer questions about your practice. As a social worker, counselor, group facilitator, or teacher, you may have frequently asked: "Am I going about my practice in the right way? Am I doing the right thing for this family, parent, or child? Am I using the right technique? Am I involving the right people in treatment? In using the techniques of program evaluation to assess your practice, you may want to make follow-up contacts with former clients to see if they still need service or to examine their status after service. Or, you might want to design a questionnaire to get quick feedback from people who attend a training program you run in your workplace.

Program evaluation techniques can tell you not only whether your practice is effective, but also in what ways your practice is or is not effective. This may tell you what changes you need to make in your practice. This is a nontraditional and an innovative, yet a simple and direct use of program evaluation techniques. Learning program evaluation to assess social programs and using techniques that help human service professionals assess their own practice are identified as two major objectives for human service professionals learning about research (Smith et al., 1986).

The following scenarios illustrate how you can use the techniques of program evaluation to help you in your practice.

APPLYING PROGRAM EVALUATION
TECHNIQUES TO YOUR OWN PRACTICE

The director of a local senior citizens center notices that the seniors come and eat their hot meal at midday but that they do not relate well to one another on a personal or social level. The seniors seem socially isolated and leave the center quickly after they eat. The director hired you as a group facilitator. For two months, you direct socialization groups. Your practice instincts tell you that group intervention is working. However, you want to find a more scientific way to determine if your practice is effective in increasing the socialization of your elderly clients. What do you do?

You work in an advocacy program for the parents of developmentally disabled children—children who are mentally retarded or autistic or who have cerebral palsy or other disabilities. The parents are poor single parents who are eligible for home-care services from the Department of Social Services, which help them raise their disabled children and ease the pressure of the daily care they give to their children. You advocate on behalf of a group of these parents and see that a homemaker is placed in their homes to help provide them some respite. You are convinced that the homemakers provide valuable service, however, you want to document the success of the service,. You do not want to evaluate the entire program, only the families that you serve. In the course of home visits to the parents, you develop ten questions that document the value of the service to them. The questions you ask are based upon the goals of the program. You use the techniques of program evaluation described in this book to help you establish the usefulness of your service.

You work in the outpatient unit of a hospital that treats dialysis patients. You are responsible for the patients' overall well-being and must see that they adhere to a strict diet and limit their intake of fluids. You wish to document whether your work is effective in helping the patients' overall condition and in helping them regulate their diets and fluid intake. You design a follow-up procedure using the techniques of program evaluation to document the success or failure of the program goals.

You treat families in a community with seriously disturbed adolescents, some of whom abused drugs. You use program evaluation techniques to design a small follow-up study and to find out how the parents thought their adolescent children were doing after treatment. By using program evaluation techniques, you are able to make assessments about the success of your treatment strategies. In addition, by interviewing enough of the parents, you find that some of the adolescents do, in fact, experience some short periods of inpatient treatment to control their drug abuse. You also find that the parents wanted more information about the possible need for short-term, inpatient treatment for their children and more information about the inpatient facilities available in their geographic area. The application of research evaluation techniques clearly helped you to improve your practice and to attend to the issue of possible short-term hospitalization for your clients.

OTHER APPLICATIONS OF THE TECHNIQUES OF PROGRAM EVALUATION

Even if your agency is not conducting evaluation research, pieces of evaluation methodology can be helpful in practice and program development. For example, you will frequently find yourself in a situation whereby your supervisor or agency executive tells you to interview clients in a program simply to find out who they are and why they participate in the program. You need to know how to design an effective data collection instrument and how to administer it. At some point in your career, you might want to look at the trends of how many times you see particular clients or you might be asked to examine service trends in your department to determine how often particular types of cases are seen. In this instance, you need a working knowledge of data analysis to ensure that you interpret the trends correctly. If a funding agency conducts an audit of your agency and selects a sample of case records on which to base its study, you need to know about sampling procedures to determine if the funding agency is taking an accurate sample of the cases in your department or agency. Knowledge about sampling procedures, then, is especially important if you wish to critique or comment on the study. This is particularly true if the study recommends budget reductions, as such audits often conclude.

As a human service professional you are expected to know program evaluation. When you submit a program proposal for outside funding, you often need to develop a plan for evaluating the program. If you know program evaluation techniques, you may be more likely to get the grant. (An example of the type of evaluation plan you might have to develop in a proposal for a training program with outside funding is described in Appendix A.)

LIMITS OF RESEARCH

Students in the human services often approach research, researchers, and research courses with much fear and trepidation. Such fear raises questions, such as, "How I will learn all the technical knowledge and the scientific methodology? Isn't research all numbers? I went into the human services to avoid mechanistic approaches toward people and social problems; isn't that what research is all about?" If you had a previous research course, I hope some of these fears were conquered. If not, be assured that this book will take a less technical, more realistic approach to research and emphasize the practical use of research.

Let it be said, however, that most concerns students have about research are, in fact, very well founded. For example, some research approaches *are* too mechanistic and often ignore subtle points in the practice process or the organizational context in which service is delivered. Some researchers *do* emphasize numbers too much, at the expense of sound problem formulation. Although they can perform elaborate statistical runs, they only ask naive questions about social problems or social programs. Some researchers also believe that simply because they conduct research they are engaged in a scientific endeavor. However, in some cases if we applied scientific criteria to some of their studies, the studies would amount to little more than journalistic accounts of people's problems or social programs.

A number of real and appropriate concerns of students are directly related to evaluation research. One major issue for students is: "How can you assess practice in the human services with numbers (empirically) when you are dealing with human beings, and there are so many variables involved?" There are all the client, family, and socioeconomic background variables, variables associated with the characteristics of the person providing the service, variables involved in the agency setting, and the many serendipitous events that happen when a person comes to a program with a problem. If you feel this way, you are right! Research only claims to measure a certain number of variables and the researcher hopes he or she is examining the right variables. Sometimes the researcher is only analyzing the associations between two variables. At other times, many variables are examined at the same time. While a good researcher is constantly on the lookout for factors that may be operating, but which are not being measured—for example, the personality of the human service practitioner—research can only study a discrete number of variables in any one study.

Another related concern is "Can all these variables be measured or translated into numbers?" While researchers are always looking to improve the measurement of concepts and variables, measurement in the social sciences is often imprecise. For example, how do you measure success in marital treatment? Is success keeping the family together or separating the family so there is less conflict? The measurement of some variables, particularly those that try to reflect practice techniques, is especially difficult to do. For example, how do you measure worker empathy? This is a variable that may be key to service delivery.

THE PURPOSE OF THIS BOOK

This book is a clear and concise guide on how to evaluate human service or counseling programs.

After reading this book and completing some of the exercises, you should be at the point where you can initiate these processes and implement small-scale program evaluations. This text will not teach you complex experimental and quasi-experimental designs or complex statistical techniques, such as regression or log-linear analysis. Instead, the purpose of this book is to provide you with the very necessary essentials of program evaluation. No previous knowledge of social science research or program evaluation is assumed.

This book is designed for students taking a course in program evaluation in the human services, social work, education, and related fields. It also is a book that people working in human service settings can read as an introduction to conducting a program evaluation. Administrators, supervisors, and practitioners working in any human service setting should find that this book offers a practical introduction to program evaluation. Because it is essentially a "how-to" book, it is different from most of the other major texts in program evaluation, such as Rossi and Freeman (1989), Tripodi (1983), or Weiss (1972). These other texts are more oriented to issues in program evaluation. They do not show the whole process of program evaluation from the beginning to the end with explicit examples. These other texts are cited in the references to this chapter, because they can be used as supplements to this text once the basic processes of program evaluation are understood.

If you have completed a course in social science research that presented the major steps in the research process, this book will help reinforce the basic research concepts. The research processes, issues, and concerns in the field of program evaluation are different. For example, you may know that the first part of the research process is where you define the research problem you wish to work on. In program evaluation, the problem for research is already specified; you ask: "How well is the program operating? How well is it achieving its goals?"

THE SIX STEPS IN PROGRAM EVALUATION

The following chapters describe program evaluation as a process that involves six steps. First, you must describe the program. Second, you need to define the program objectives. Third, you design the study by choosing a design, deciding how to collect data, constructing a data collection instrument, and selecting a sample. Fourth, you need to implement the study by collecting data about the program. Fifth, you need to analyze the data you have collected. Sixth, you report the results of your program evaluation. The emphasis in this book will be on how to conduct program evaluation by following these six steps.

The second chapter explains the importance of program evaluation and provides a comprehensive definition of program evaluation as a research methodology, as practice, as politics, and as a field of research. In the following chapters, each step in program evaluation is described. The third chapter describes the first step in the process—defining the program. The last section of that chapter describes how you may use evaluation research to conduct a needs-assessment study. The fourth chapter explains the second step of how to define program goals. The last section of that chapter indicates how you may use evaluation techniques to conduct program monitoring and provides an example of how you can operationalize program goals in a child welfare training program.

The third step, designing the study, is described in the fifth chapter. It describes how to choose a research design, how to formulate a data collection strategy, how to construct a data collection instrument, and how to select a sample. A case example of a data collection instrument that was used for evaluating an Employee Assistance Program is described after the section on constructing a data collection instrument. The fourth step, implementing the evaluation, and the fifth step, analyzing the data, are described in the sixth chapter. Examples of both quantitative and qualitative data analysis are presented in that chapter. The sixth and last step, conclusions, implications and recommendations, and reporting the results of program evaluation are described in the final chapter.

SUMMARY OF KEY IDEAS IN THIS CHAPTER

These are the key points you should remember from this chapter:

1. Questions about the effects of social programs are important for you to have as a caring human service professional.
2. On a program level, program evaluation is used to assess the program design, program implementation, and program usefulness and impact. On

a practice level, the techniques of program evaluation can be applied to determine the effectiveness of your interventions.

3. Program evaluation techniques are important for you to learn as a human service professional. In your career, you may be asked to oversee an evaluation study, to initiate and implement program evaluation, or to develop a plan for evaluation as part of a funding proposal.

4. It is also important to learn pieces of evaluation research. For example, learning program evaluation helps you understand how to develop program goals, how to design data collection instruments, and how to assess the planning and implementation of social programs.

5. The research process has inherent limitations, for example, the unresolved measurement issues in the social sciences. Nevertheless, human service professionals need to maintain a commitment to program evaluation.

6. There are six steps in program evaluation as presented in this book. First, you must describe the program. Second, you need to define the program objectives. Third, you design the study by choosing a design, deciding how to collect data, constructing a data collection instrument, and selecting a sample. Fourth, you need to implement the study by collecting data about the program. Fifth, you need to analyze the data you have collected. Sixth, you report the results of your program evaluation.

EXERCISES FOR THIS CHAPTER

1. List and discuss evaluative questions you have about a human service program you know about.

2. For a program you know about, develop separate questions related to the program plan or design, questions related to the program implementation and operations, and questions about the program outcome or impact.

REFERENCES

Rossi, P.H., & Freeman, H.E. (1989). *Evaluation: A systematic approach.* Beverly Hills, CA: Sage Publications Inc.

Smith, M.L., DeWeaver, K., & Kilpatrick, A.C. (1986). Research curricula and accreditation: The challenge for leadership. *Journal of Social Work Education,* (2) 61–70.

Tripodi, T. (1983). *Evaluative research for social workers.* Englewood Cliffs, NJ: Prentice-Hall.

Weiss, C.H. (1972). *Evaluation research: Methods of assessing program effectiveness.* Englewood Cliffs, NJ: Prentice-Hall.

2 A Comprehensive Definition of Program Evaluation

An evaluation is a judgment, and judgments are common in everyday life. We are constantly making judgments. What time should we get up? What should we eat for breakfast? Should we eat the food in the school cafeteria? What school should I send my children to? Should I take the job or not? Whom should I choose as a mate? Should I go for therapy or personal counseling?

We can actually think about making a judgment in our personal lives based upon a research methodology. Let's take the question of who you might live with or marry. You could formulate a research question: "Should I marry Harry or not?" Then you go out and collect data. You might observe Harry in social situations to see if he has the personal and interpersonal characteristics you might like. You observe your close interactions with Harry. You talk to your friends about Harry. Some family counseling professionals even suggest you structure the data collection process a little more. You might go for a weekend with Harry to visit one of his relatives. You might go for a weekend to relatives who have children and take care of the children together to see how you relate to and discipline children together. Then, based upon your observations and the data you collected, you analyze that data and arrive at a conclusion—You will marry Harry or you will not marry Harry. Of course, real life is based upon less structured and less formalistic judgments, but this is how a research process could be used to help you with this personal judgment.

14

Judgments and evaluations are also part of our professional lives. Our supervisors at work make judgments about our abilities and skills. We judge the types of service that are right for particular people who want our services. We constantly formulate evaluations or diagnoses about the children, families, parents, adults, and others whom we try to help. We also judge whether what we do has the right effect. For example, we might ask: "Is this particular teaching technique working with this group of students?"

Sometimes professional evaluative processes have pieces that look like research. For example, in evaluating staff in an organization, the administrator might give supervisors a scale on which to rate their staff in terms of professional demeanor, practice skills, and so forth. However, this is not evaluative research. These ratings are not part of a larger research study in which a research question is formulated and the principles of social science research are applied. Also, the administrator is not assessing the reliability of these ratings using the systematic methods of social science.

What makes these evaluative processes in our personal and professional lives different from evaluation research? Research uses the systematic, standardized methods of social science to assess social interventions and social programs. These methods help us formulate an evaluative research question, guide us in observing and collecting data that will help us answer the question, and provide us with principles on how to analyze data once we have collected the data.

DEFINITION OF PROGRAM EVALUATION

Program evaluation is the use of social science research methods by evaluators, administrators, or practitioners to assess the planning, implementation, or outcome of social programs in a political environment.

Note that there are four parts to this definition. First, program evaluation employs a social science *research methodology*. Second, there are people— evaluators, administrators, or practitioners—who engage in the *practice of evaluation research*. Third, program evaluation is a broad *field of research*, in which the researcher can engage in a wide variety of studies, such as planning studies, monitoring studies, and studies that assess whether the program achieves its goals. Fourth, evaluation is *political*. We will address each of these parts of program evaluation separately—program evaluation as methodology, program evaluation as practice, program evaluation as a field of research, and program evaluation as politics.

Program Evaluation As a Research Methodology

The systematic methods and principles of social science research help us reduce error when they are applied correctly. The methods guide us in what research questions to ask, how to observe and collect data, how to obtain reliable and valid data, who to interview, how to construct an interview, how to interview people, how to analyze their responses, what statistical procedures to use, and so on.

As with the principles in other fields of study, they can be applied poorly throughout the study, very well throughout the study, or poorly in some areas but well in others. For example, the researcher might formulate a good research question and develop a questionnaire that collects reliable and valid data, but he or she might only interview the people who continued with the program and neglect to interview those who dropped out. In other words, the researcher may have a biased sample. The researcher might use the proper statistical techniques to analyze the data but he or she might use data that were unreliable, because the questionnaire was poorly worded and the data were collected in a haphazard fashion.

The value of social science methods is the framework they provide in helping us judge whether the principles of problem formulation, design, sampling, data collection, and data analysis are applied correctly. Most often we find that a particular piece of research is systematic and applies the principles of social science research in some areas, but less systematic in other areas. Research methods are important, because they provide a *standardized framework* within which we critique how well research methods are used in a particular evaluation study. In other words, viewing a program from a standardized framework means that the person looking at an evaluation can determine how well research criteria are met. For example, did the researcher ask leading questions that skewed the conclusions with favorable results? We can look at his or her questionnaire to see if this was the case. Or, did the researcher select only a sample of people to interview who completed the program, and did he or she neglect to interview those people who did not complete the program and might have more negative attitudes toward the program? We can examine the researcher's sampling plan to determine if there was a representative sample or an *average* group of people who used the program. Or, we may find that the sampling plan was good and reliable data were collected, but that the wrong statistical technique was used and the data analysis was flawed. Examining the evaluation within a standard framework of how well research methods are applied means that it is possible to be "relatively" more objective about the program.

Social science research methods provide us with the tools for reducing error in problem formulation, design, sampling, data collection, and data analysis. This is what distinguishes evaluation research from other personal and professional evaluative processes. While some evaluative processes look like research—i.e., a structured rating scale used to evaluate professional staff—they are not research if they do not follow the principles of how to formulate a research problem, how to observe or collect data, how to analyze data, and so forth.

What role do the researcher's own values play in these scientific processes? If the researcher values or devalues the intervention, these values may affect his or her ability to apply the standard methods of social science in an objective manner. In fact, the values of all parties involved in the program definitely affect how the program evaluation is planned and what types of research questions are asked. A helpful process in planning evaluative research is to have all the parties involved—the researcher, the administrators, the practitioners—declare their values relative to the program. For example, do they like the program? Do they value the practice methods that are being used? The more we understand the values of these different parties, the more clearly we can determine to what degree values may affect the standardized methodology.

Program Evaluation As Practice

To many people, program evaluation is chiefly a research methodology. Most texts in program evaluation discuss the application of social science research methodology as the key aspect of evaluation. However, program evaluation is much more. Program evaluation is a practice methodology within the human services, similar to other practice methodologies, such as personal counseling, family counseling, group work practice, and so forth.

Program evaluation provides a service to organizations, agencies, and institutions that use evaluation well. The person who engages in evaluation research can help the administrators and practitioners in organizations in a number of simple but effective ways. What is the nature of research as service? Evaluation research can help an agency keep its commitment to its mission and to the goals and objectives of its programs at all stages of program development. The researcher can help the organization sort out programming and research issues.

For example, the person engaged in evaluation research often begins by helping the organization generate comprehensive descriptions of the program and the interventive methods it will use. In planning the program evaluation, the evaluator specifies the larger context in which the program operates by reviewing the literature and by examining those methods shown to be effective in different types of programs as reported in the literature. The program evaluator also may help the practitioners explicate the practice principles being used in a particular program. The person engaged in evaluation research may help the administrators and program staff think through the rationale for the program and clarify the goals and objectives of the particular program. Furthermore, the researcher can help people in the organization assess which program goals are plausible and which are less likely to be achieved given the type of level or intervention.

The practice of evaluation research means that the researcher must form a helping relationship with administrators and staff to assist the agency. The researcher must possess human relations skills and personal characteristics that make people feel comfortable, not threatened. To help the organization, the researcher should engage staff at all levels. The researcher, too, benefits from the relationship by gaining greater understanding of the organization and of the program being evaluated.

Lewis has discussed the need for awareness of the value of human relations skills and the researcher's *use of self* in a practice role:

> In the beginning phase of the study, [the researcher] must examine the timeliness and appropriateness of [what] the agency wishes to have studied. [He] must assure agency participation in the question to be studied. He is expected to prepare and involve the appropriate persons whose assistance he will need to obtain his data.... In writing the report, he will have to provide for the agency's critical review.... (Lewis, 1959, p. 17)

Very often you hear of program evaluators who are accused, especially by practice staff, of not understanding the true nature of a particular program. The practice staff may feel left out of the particular study. All they do is complete administrative forms about the program, but no one asks them what the program is all about. By treating program evaluation as a practice method it is possible for the researcher to be more sensitive about taking into account the opinions of various members of the organization.

When evaluation research is defined purely as method, the person doing evaluation may choose not to be involved in the program so as to remain more "objective." Defining program evaluation as a practice method means that program evaluation represents much more than designing the study, collecting the data, analyzing the data, drawing conclusions and writing the report. Each part of the research process may be valued when we define program evaluation as practice.

A story was told to me about a famous social work researcher who said that when she conducted a program evaluation for an agency, she usually started by designing a study. During the initial few weeks at the agency, she would meet with the executive staff, who would say, "The real problem here is that we do not have enough workers or the right kind of workers to give adequate service." Then she would go to lunch with the practitioners, who would say, "The problem is the executives. There is no leadership. They will not give us the kind of support we need to provide adequate service." She found that it was her job to explain that she was hired to do a particular program evaluation. She had to move administrative and practice staff from their immediate concerns to the focus of the study. She discovered that the research plan becomes the contract of what the researcher must achieve. She also learned that her personality was very important in achieving her goals and that she had to remain aware of the attitudes and personalities of those involved.

Defining program evaluation as a service and a practice methodology means that you accept the view that research is more than simply learning and applying research methods. The researcher is a caring person. He or she cares about the organization, its mission, its staff at all levels, its politics, its clients and the larger community, the sponsorship for the program, and the program itself.

Program Evaluation As a Field of Research

Program evaluation is a field of research in which the methods of social science research are used to assess social interventions and social programs. Usually, program evaluation is goal- or outcome-oriented evaluation. Evaluation is used, in this instance, to establish whether program outcomes are achieved. However, outcome-oriented evaluations are not the only types of program evaluation. The field of program evaluation includes the techniques used to evaluate the need for the program, the techniques for documenting and describing program operations, as well as the ultimate outcomes and goals.

Studies that evaluate the need for the program and the program concept or rationale are called *needs-assessment studies.* Needs-assessement studies evaluate the need for the program and the program concept. These studies usually are conducted when the program is being planned. They do not evaluate program operations or outcomes.

If you were planning an after-school child care program in your community, you might conduct a survey of community residents to see if they would use such a program. Also, you could review data from the U.S. Bureau of the Census on family characteristics in that community to establish the need for the after-school program. Both of these are examples of needs-assessment studies. While the research question differs in needs-assessment studies, the methods used are similar to traditional outcome-oriented evaluation. For example, you would need to know how to select a sample of people to be interviewed, how to construct a questionnaire, how to analyze data, and how to interpret the results. Needs-assessment studies are discussed in Chapter 3.

Program monitoring studies are evaluative studies in which the methods of social science are used to assess *how the program intervention is operating.* In monitoring studies, more emphasis is placed upon feedback about the intervention rather than upon a formal assessment of whether program goals are achieved. A survey of the clients' perceptions about service, or a survey of agency staff to see how they describe the program, or a descriptive study of the interventions of some professionals in the program are examples of program-monitoring studies.

Program-monitoring studies that describe more fully how the program works or its *process* are sometimes called *process evaluations.* Process evaluations often use some type of direct observation of the program to find out how it works. Monitoring studies that examine the economic costs associated with the intervention are called *cost studies.* Sometimes cost studies also examine program goals or outcomes, in which case they are called *cost-benefit studies.* Program-monitoring studies are discussed in Chapter 4.

This is a broad view of program evaluation, which includes a variety of processes. Program evaluation can be defined more narrowly as the use of research to assess whether the program achieves its goals. However, as a field of endeavor, program evaluation is much broader. It includes program monitoring, or the monitoring of program operations through the use of research strategies. It includes process evaluation, or the evaluation of the interventive process with less emphasis on outcomes or goals than that associated with "pure" program evaluation. It includes cost studies that determine the cost of social programs and assess their benefits. It also includes studies that assess the initial and ongoing needs of the program. It includes program monitoring, process evaluation, cost-benefit analysis, and needs-assessment studies.

Program evaluation is the application of standardized social science research methodology during the planning phase of social programs through needs-assessment studies, during the implementation phase of social programs through monitoring and cost studies, and later through goal-oriented program evaluation. Program evaluation leads to reality-based program planning and assessment based upon data collected using the methods of social science.

Program Evaluation As Politics

The evaluation researcher also is involved in the *politics* of the agency or institution in which he or she conducts the research. If the researcher ignores the politics of research, he or she will be less effective. Just as the need for program evaluation will never go away, the politics of evaluation research will always be there.

Social programs are political, and program evaluation by its very nature takes place in a political decision-making environment. The political nature of social programs is described best by Freeman and Rossi (1989). They say that interventions compete with each other for funds from foundations, international organizations, and the various levels of government. Similarly, specific interventions within programs often compete for funds and resources. Choices must be made continually between funding and not funding, continuing or discontinuing, and expanding or contracting one program as opposed to another.

Weiss describes evaluation as a "rational enterprise that takes place in a political context" (1987, p. 47). She cites three major ways in which political considerations are present. First, social programs are created by political decisions. The programs are subject to both supportive and hostile political pressures. Second, evaluation feeds into political decision making. Evaluation competes with other factors that carry weight in the political process. Third, evaluation itself is a political enterprise that takes political stances. For example, evaluation reports usually indicate that "the program needs improving;" "it needs major overhauls;" "the program is working fine." This points to the role of the social scientist in program and policy formation.

What role does evaluation research play in program and policy formation? Usually research plays less of a role than the political process itself. Most of the decisions made in the organization are political decisions made by upper-echelon staff. To some executives, having a job with power and resources is more important than any programming issue or how services affect clients. People are sometimes more interested in saving their own jobs than in exposing any weaknesses in their programs. So, why do evaluation? The administrators' pet projects will be considered valuable, despite the conclusions of evaluation research. Administrators often hire internal researchers who give them the results they want or who look positively on their programs or who bury critical findings.

The political process always takes precedence over and control of the research process. However, the fact that research uses a standard method that can give you a more objective orientation than the executive *fiat* is a crucial consideration. Research also can be used to create a balance by representing the experiences of clients and staff in the agency decision-making process. Ultimately, we need proof of the degree to which our programs are working or not working. Although research, like any other method, can be abused, often we find it *can* make a difference in the political process if it is used properly.

> The evaluation gamble in an imperfect world is that data can make a difference; that some scientific logic and attention to empirical reality is better than none; and that some . . . grounding in and concern for empirically derived judgments is better than a world of pure unadulterated politics based entirely on might. (Patton, 1987, p. 103)

WHY EVALUATION RESEARCH IS NEEDED

There are four key reasons we do program evaluation: to enhance belief systems, accountability, knowledge building, and consumerism.

Professionals in the human services *believe* in what they do. For example, a person leading a group of elderly residents in a nursing home needs to believe in the purposes of that group in order to have the drive and commitment necessary to serve people. Researchers often note that persons providing direct service tend to be very enthusiastic about what they do and how they do it. This commitment may be crucial in implementing a particular service strategy. Of course, energy and commitment are not enough. So, people who provide direct services learn professional skills as they continue to provide service, either through formal education or through training given at the agency.

Belief systems are important. In fact, there is a body of research suggesting that hopefulness in practice improves the results (Polansky & Kent, 1978). However, enthusiasm, education and skill are still not enough. We need to know how programs work and whether they achieve results. Many have criticized professionals in the human services for being "do-gooders." Blind benevolence is not what is needed. If you are employed in a job-training program, or a foster care agency, or a community settlement house, or a family counseling agency, or a child guidance, or youth agency, it is not sufficient to believe in what you are doing. You also must think about the program and try to determine whether it is achieving its goals.

The best human service workers are not those who simply believe in what they do, but are those who frequently question it to arrive at better practice. Whether they know it or not, these practitioners have incorporated some of the attitudes and skills of program evaluators in their work. Skill can only take us so far, we also need to study the structural arrangements in service delivery. For example, what if you have a successful curriculum for job training and have very skillful job trainers, but the program is not recruiting the type of youth who can most benefit from it? Skill in practice is not enough to mount a successful program. One way in which we cultivate a better picture of programs and how they work is through research that looks intensively at social programs—that is, evaluation research.

Human service professionals have a tremendous responsibility to provide satisfactory, reasonable justification for the services they provide, that is, to be accountable. To whom are we accountable? First and foremost, we are accountable to the clients to whom we provide service. Second, as ethical practitioners, we need to be accountable to ourselves. Third, we are accountable to supervisors, administrators, and the employing institution or agency. Fourth, we are accountable to funding sources, the various branches of government or the voluntary sector that support our institution or agency.

Fifth, we are accountable to the community we serve or the one in which our program is located.

It is crucial that we realize that the need for accountability will never go away. One social agency I know has so far avoided the accountability issue. This agency operates a volunteer student program in which college students volunteer their time to help people. The administrators and practitioners of this program *believe* that the volunteers will benefit from it. They also believe that many volunteers will go into human service professions when they graduate from college. Administrators know about one or two "success stories," but have never conducted evaluation research to determine the type of effect the program has on the majority of student-volunteers. Every year this program is faced with renewal of funding. Whenever questions about the success of the program arise, administrators and executive staff can only discuss those one or two cases that are already known in vivid detail as successes. To be able to account satisfactorily for the program, they need to proceed beyond these one or two success stories to document the benefits for a small group of volunteers, or, better yet, for all the volunteers in the program. Notice that in this example the evaluation question did not go away, although no one knows whether the program is working. And because no one knows, they are risking eventual termination of their funding.

When human service professionals act as if evaluation is not important, it appears as though they do not care about the results of programs. Let's take the example of two social workers at a board meeting. A board member who is a successful businessmen is accustomed to seeing results in clear form: increase in sales, increased profits, and so on. This board member argues for more evaluation of the agency's efforts. In contrast, one human service professional states that it is impossible to evaluate human service programs because results are too difficult to measure, there are too many variables involved when you talk about human beings, etcetera. Another human service professional presents an alternate point of view. Although conceding the difficulty of program evaluation, this professional argues that it needs to be done. The stance of the first professional is an untenable one. What is the alternative to program evaluation. There is none. Who would say that the professional's efforts cannot be evaluated? Yet, in a sense, this is the situation for social agencies that fail to take evaluation seriously.

Program evaluation provides us with *knowledge about programming efforts* and about how well social problems are being solved. We can document the positive outcomes in programs that *do* work. Similarly, we can document the reasons why some programs do not work. Unfortunately, the level of social programming is often naive and rudimentary. For example, there are programs that say they will cure alcoholism or drug abuse with 10 contacts by a social worker. Such programs could benefit from program evaluation.

One example of a poorly planned program is a summer camp program for single parents and their children, which I evaluated. The children of single parents attended a camp program with their counselors. A major part of the program also involved discussion groups for the parents to talk about the issues of single parenting. The parents' part of the program was poorly planned and the groups stopped meeting in the first few days of camp. An administrator from the agency staff visited the camp to improve matters, but was unsuccessful. At a meeting held at the conclusion of the program, the administrator told the researchers: "You can let us have it on this program. We really messed up." I wrote a report to reflect the program's weaknesses.

After reading the report, the administrator telephoned me and began by saying: "You son of a bitch." One of his concerns was that the researchers failed to report on a major part of the social intervention. What was this intervention? A softball game. He was involved in the game, playing on the team opposite the single parents. He played catcher, and when the single parents came close to crossing home plate to score a run, he let them score. He believed that the report should reflect the *feeling* that was generated between the single parents and the agency as a result of this *intervention*. This was the type of programming valued by this administrator of a large social welfare agency with a multimillion dollar budget.

The degree to which we document better programming efforts means that we can create a knowledge base of program interventions. The human services field has a unique contribution to make in being especially attentive to processes of service delivery and variables in program intervention. Researchers can sometimes be guilty of treating the program as a "black box" (Weiss, 1972). They are interested only in program outcomes, not in program processes. These researchers may not recognize that evaluative research promotes knowledge-building in program interventions.

Program evaluation leads to better program planning. The middle-range planning gains from using program evaluation techniques are often the most salient reasons for engaging in evaluation research. For example:

1. Trying to measure program goals leads to greater understanding of the program and its goals.
2. The need to describe a program for purposes of evaluation means that a more comprehensive description of the program will be written.
3. Developing a questionnaire in which you ask consumers about the intervention helps you conceptualize the program more clearly.
4. After the study is conducted, program planners, supervisors, and administrators meet to discuss *specific* evaluative findings, rather than typical program planning meetings in which programs are described in vague terms.

Program evaluation also promotes *consumerism* in that the recipients of programs are asked directly about the usefulness of programs. It tests whether recipients of service gain from the services and what they think of the services. We are in an age of consumerism, therefore all power is not in the hands of the professional. In program evaluation, too often we see professionals "blaming the victim," blaming the clients for not using services that "we thought" could help them (Ryan, 1971). Consumers of programs can be empowered through program evaluation. As a simple example, clients in an agency that routinely conducts evaluation by asking them about the service and about their perspective on the results of the service have a greater voice in program planning than do consumers who receive service from a program that fails to evaluate its program in this manner. Clients are empowered when their opinions and feelings about the service are fedback into program planning.

SUMMARY OF KEY IDEAS IN THIS CHAPTER

1. An evaluation is a judgment.

2. Program evaluation is the use of social science research methods by evaluators, administrators, or practitioners to assess the planning, implementation, or outcomes of social programs.

3. Program evaluation is a research methodolgy. Evaluation uses the systematic, standardized methods of social science to assess social interventions and social programs. The methods of social science research provide a framework within which we can assess social programs. The quality of a program evaluation study can be assessed by how well it adheres to the accepted methods of social science.

4. Program evaluation is a practice methodology. It provides a service to organizations through better descriptions of programs and better program planning. The researcher's relationship skills are essential in the practice of program evaluation.

5. Program evaluation is a field of research that includes needs-assessment studies, program-monitoring studies, cost studies, cost-benefit studies, process studies, and outcome-oriented research studies.

6. Program evaluation is inherently political. Program evaluation *can* make a difference; however, political decisions will always affect social programs much more than program evaluation.

7. Program evaluation is essential if we care about enhancing belief systems, increased accountability, creating new knowledge about social programs, and promoting consumerism.

EXERCISES FOR THIS CHAPTER

1. Indicate, on a personal level, whether you believe in what you do. How might you add to this belief through evaluation research?

2. Choose a program you know about. Indicate its major issues in terms of belief systems, accountability, knowledge-building and consumerism.

REFERENCES

Lewis, H. (1959). The place of the research project in the Master's curriculum. In *Selected papers in methods of teaching research in the social work curriculum*. New York: Council on Social Work Education.

Patton, M.Q. (1987). Evaluation's political inherency: Practical implications for design and use. In D. Palumbo (Ed.), *The politics of program evaluation* (p. 103). Newberry Park, CA: Sage Publications.

Rossi, P.H., & Freeman, H.E. (1989). *Evaluation: A systematic approach*. Beverly Hills, CA: Sage Publications.

Polansky, N.A., & Kent, M.L. (1978). Troubled people. In H.S. Mass (Ed.), *Social service research: Reviews of studies* (pp. 158-159). Washington, DC: National Association of Social Workers.

Ryan, W. (1971). *Blaming the victim*. New York: Pantheon Books.

Weiss, C.H. (1987). Where politics and evaluation research meet. In D. Palumbo (Ed.), *The politics of program evaluation* (pp. 47–48). Newberry Park, CA: Sage Publications.

Weiss, C.H. (1972). *Evaluation research: Method of assessing program effectiveness* (p. 43). Englewood Cliffs, NJ: Prentice-Hall.

3 The First Step: Describing the Program

Social scientists usually discuss three main purposes for social science research methods. First, there is *exploration,* or the use of social research to gain a beginning insight into a social phenomenon. Second, there is *description,* in which the purpose is to describe situations and events through careful and deliberate observation. Third, there is *prediction,* wherein the goal is to predict social phenomena (Babbie, 1986).

Social programs are very complex. Achieving prediction of certain outcomes as a result of the program is often not possible. However, program evaluation does use the techniques of social science to explore and describe social phenomena. The *exploration* and *description* of social programs and interventions is extremely valuable. An important effect of evaluation research is producing better descriptions of social programs.

It is important to describe the program. Describing the program may be the most critical part of program evaluation. Comprehensive descriptions of social programming efforts may be more important than looking at the goals of the program. Suppose the researcher carried out an evaluation in which he or she did not bother to describe the different parts of the program? The researcher found that the program achieved its goals. But what caused the program to be successful? Was it the skills of the staff? Was it the way in which the program recruited people? Was it because the clients served had so many needs? Without sound and comprehensive descriptions of the program we do not know what leads to its success or failure.

We need to describe programs fully before we can add incrementally to the knowledge base of social programming and program development.

Otherwise, we will be unable to achieve one of the most important values of program evaluation, that is, knowledge-building about social interventions. Also, if people in the setting do not know what the program is and how it operates, how can they engage in making the program better?

Furthermore, if the program is successful, we want to ensure that it could be *replicated* or *reproduced* so that other agencies and institutions can benefit from the lessons learned. We can only replicate programs if we have detailed and comprehensive program descriptions.

Explorations and descriptions of social programs also are important because programs change over time. Social programs are action endeavors that take place in action settings. What the program was planned to be may be very different than what the program has become in its first year of implementation. Program goals and processes may have changed greatly. Formal goals of the program may no longer be actual goals if one examines day-to-day program operations. There can be discrepancies between what the program is and what the program should be. Conflict resolution may be needed if the administrator thinks the program is being carried out one way, when in fact it is being implemented in a different manner.

Programs are not strictly quantifiable entities. Parts of social programs may be quantifiable, such as the number of times the service provider meets with the service recipient, or how much one unit of service costs, or the sociodemographic characteristics of the people who receive the service. One may create a checklist of the problems that bring a person for service, thereby learning that a person came for help with a consumer problem or for help in finding day care, but this checklist cannot detail the person's specific request or the process by which the service provider attempts to help that person. Factors such as the philosophical base of practice or the different interpretations practitioners have of the program are often impossible to quantify. You need qualitative program descriptions to help you identify the components of the program.

Because social programs also are very complex phenomena, descriptions of the program are crucial. Weiss defines a program as "an amalgam of dreams, personalities, theories and assumptions, rooms, paper clips, organizational structures, clients and activities, photo copies, budgets and great intentions" (Weiss, 1972, p. 43). Given that a program has many amorphous qualities, one purpose of program evaluation is the exploration and description of the relevant programmatic and client variables that lead to its success.

For research purposes, we not only need quantitative methods to measure the measurable parts of the program, but we also need qualitative methods to examine program processes and operations and descriptive outcomes.

METHODS FOR DESCRIBING THE PROGRAM

How does the researcher go about describing the program? You might expect that you would merely have to consult the organization's written description of the program. WRONG!!! First of all, it is surprising how often the written description of the program is inadequate. Frequently, everyone assumes they know what they are doing. People start implementing the program, but no one takes the time to describe the program. Sometimes the program description is so poorly written, you cannot tell what the program is by reading it. In other cases, you may find an adequately written description of the program. This happens particularly when the program is funded outside the organization and a proposal about the program has to be written or if the organization itself requires a formal planning effort before the program can be initiated. As a rule of thumb, the more program planning is done, the more likely a program description is available. The more program planning is done, the better and more thorough the program description will be.

If there is a formal description of the program, the researcher has to be wary. How do you know the program is what the description says it is? At this point the researcher needs to use qualitative methods to explore and describe the program. He or she should observe the program in operation. It also is necessary to interview key administrators, supervisors, teachers, social workers, and others about the program. Those receiving the service also should be interviewed. In these interviews, the researcher should ask general questions about what the program is, how it operates, who the program serves, what methods are used, what funds are available for the program, and what are the important aspects fo the program. Where differences of opinion exist, these should be noted. Then, based upon the consensus of opinion about the program, the researcher should write a program description.

It is crucial for the researcher to investigate the program in this manner. You do not merely want to accept people's word about what the program is. You do not want to accept the administrator's view, or the teacher's view, or the social worker's view, or the client's view of the program.

Note that at this point you are not fully implementing the evaluation. You research the program so that you can describe the program and the key issues associated with the program. You interview one person or two persons in the categories of administrator, service provider, client, and so forth.

Note that you use research methodologies, observation, and interviewing, to generate a more inclusive description of the program than would normally exist. Scientific method is used for descriptive purposes. If the program is at an initial point or if not much program planning exists, it is possible that the observational processes and interviews with key parties involved in the program could become the whole evaluation. In this case, the researcher could do a more descriptive, exploratory evaluation of the program, with more formal interviews of the parties involved and a more rigorous plan for observing the program in operation and for analyzing the data. The researcher could also do a monitoring study based upon direct observation of the program in operation.

These methods for creating the program description are similar to the methods others have suggested for use in *evaluability assessment* studies (Rossi & Freeman, 1989). Evaluability assessment studies are pre-evaluation studies that assess the program and the agency climate to determine if a program evaluation study can be conducted. These studies often use qualitative research methods to interview program staff and observe the program. The evaluator also consults formal descriptions of the program and tries to build an evaluable program model.

WRITING THE PROGRAM DESCRIPTION

The next step for the researcher is to write a description of the program based upon consensus opinion. While there are some standardized methods for collecting data about the program, i.e., interview key people, observe the program, ask about program operations, and so on, there is more flexibility in how to *write* the program description. One needs to consult written descriptions of the program, observational notes about the program in operation, and interviews conducted with those involved with the program. Then outline or write the program description. While guidelines for writing the description are more flexible, there are some standard areas of social programming. Although the following is a suggested list, it is not necessary that every program area be addressed. The researcher should ensure that some of the basic descriptive areas are covered.

List of Suggested Content in the Program Description

1. An Overview of the Program and the Program Rationale.
2. The Interventive Methods Used.
3. Key Elements in the Program Field or Context.
4. The Setting Where the Program is Being Conducted.
5. Program Funding and Cost.
6. The Clients or Consumers Served.
7. Characteristics of the Staff Providing Service.
8. Implementation Issues.

Each of these areas might be a separate section of the program description.

1. *An Overview of the Program and the Program Rationale.*
The researcher must look at the need the program was designed to meet or the social problem the program was to correct. In other words, what is the general purpose of the program? Which social problem does the program address? What rationale is the program based upon? Is this a critical problem of the day that demands our attention no matter how limited our program efforts? For example, a program to help support AIDS patients in the community through the help of volunteers addresses a timely and significant problem. This program addresses a problem that will not go away, so we want to improve program efforts in that area, even if the program effort is not successful, because something needs to be done. Thus, we are more likely to be tolerant of some failure if the program attempts to meet significant social need. On the other hand, we must watch out for fadism. Merely because the social problem is current and receives attention in the media, the program may still be unsuccessful. For example, an agency administrator might say, "Let's do something in the area of homelessness," without doing an adequate planning job.

At this initial point, we need to know the intervention planned and how it will affect or change the situation. What theories, principles, and assumptions of practice is the program based upon? Are those principles logical? In this general description of the program, we need to include initial statements that consider: In what type of setting is the program located? Who will fund or sponsor the program? Who will receive service? About how many people will be served? From where will clients be recruited? How much will it cost?

This overview statement is important whether you are evaluating a new or long-established program. The overview is important for two reasons. First, the overview-description must include the program rationale, the problem the program is designed to correct, and the purpose of the program. This is crucial because the development of the program's goals and objectives—which is the second step in program evaluation—should follow from the general statement of what the program is trying to achieve. Second, these general descriptions of the program, the setting, the funding, the numbers of people served, and so on are a prelude to the additional areas that will be examined in more detail later in the program description.

2. *The Interventive Methods Used.*
We need to know what methods are proposed to achieve the program's results: Counseling, individual treatment, group methods, training or teaching, methods of organizing or mobilizing people? Are we giving people money, benefits, or a service or educating them? Within each particular

method, what are the principles of practice? If counseling methods are being used, is it reality therapy, analytic therapy, or short-term treatment? What theories or assumptions lay behind the intervention used? Is there a logic to how the program could reasonably use its interventive methods to achieve its goals? What does the interventive literature say about using the particular intervention? Has it been used with this particular group of clients before? Has it been shown to be successful in correcting this particular problem? How might the method affect the changes being sought? How will it work in operation? Are staff committed to the particular intervention used?

The length and time of service should be described: How many hours per day, days per week, and over how long a period of time? What day of the week? Will it be planned during the day although most of the parents probably will be working? Will the program be provided at the right time in their life cycle? For example, if a program is planned for single parents, their needs six months after the divorce may be quite different from their needs three years after the divorce. If the program is designed to prevent certain problems, will the intervention occur before the problem is so serious they cannot be helped? For example, if the program is to prevent children from being placed in foster care, will the situations of the families being served be so serious that nothing can be done? Have people or families been recruited at the right point in time?

Are there conflicts among staff about the interventions that should be used? For example, the clinical director of a drug rehabilitation program may feel that attendance at a particular group program should be compulsory while the staff may feel it should be optional. Staff may believe that the group program duplicates their work in individual therapy and, therefore, is not necessary, while the clinical director believes it is essential. Or, family therapists in a program may think that the whole family needs to come for therapy before it can be effective, while other practitioners think family involvement is unnecessary.

3. Key Elements of the Program Field or Context.

In describing the program, we should describe the context of this particular program. This means where does the program fit in terms of the sponsoring organization and the local community, the city, the state, the nation? What is the program area or field of service? What is the "state of the art" in that particular field of service. The researcher needs to examine similar types of programs and review the literature in terms of both program descriptions and other evaluation studies. The researcher needs to put the program in a broader context and report how this particular program is different or similar to other program efforts. Which strategies have proven successful in the past in such programs and which interventions have not worked? What are the success rates for particular kinds of outcomes being achieved? Is it generally difficult or easy to achieve these outcomes? Which issues in program implementation have usually surfaced?

For example, if you are planning an employee assistance program, you would relate the program to particular types of EAP program models. If you are planning a "broad-brush" program—which provides a variety of counseling and advocacy services to help people with personal problems, consumer problems, or help in finding a nursing home for a relative or a day care service—you would assess the "state of the art" in "broad-brush" programs. If you were planning an employee assistance program that used a drug and alcohol model, you would relate your program to the literature in this programming area. You would examine both descriptions of programs and the evaluation literature on EAP programs related to substance abuse. Even the rationale for choosing a broad-brush or a substance abuse focus would be an important issue in this program context, and the selection of one or the other program format should be thoroughly researched in the literature.

The importance of assessing the broader context is illustrated by one of my former students. He was evaluating a program to match senior citizens who needed housing with people in the community who had rental apartments available in their homes. In conducting the evaluation, he found that the program made successful matches for only 10% of the cases registered. One might think that a 50% success rate would be needed to consider these programs effective. However, the student put the program in its larger context by reviewing the literature evaluating such programs and found that the *usual* success rate in these programs was 10 to 15%. If the number of matches of seniors to housing is substantial and the matching process is not costly, a 15% matching rate might be acceptable.

4. *The Setting Where the Program is Being Conducted.*
Where will the program be located physically? In what type of organization? What is the structure of that organization? Does the organization have a bureaucratic structure with rules and regulations that interfere with the community-based focus of the program? What management issues are involved in running the program? What is the history of the program within the organization? Is it the administrator's pet program? What political issues are there in the program setting? What is the auspice of the organization in which the program is located? Is it a public or private institution? Is it sectarian? What is the history of the organization? Has history shown that the service seems more or less successful?

Some authors in evaluation research recommend a *systems approach* to evaluation, whereby some of these larger issues about the organizational setting are examined exclusively (Etzioni, 1960). The systems model views the organization as an organism that has certain needs and must perform certain functions to survive. For example, the organization needs funds, resources, and clients. It must relate to the larger community. Departments within the organization must relate to one another, and so on. All these factors can affect a program's implementation *and* its ability to achieve its goals. A whole evaluative study could be designed around the role of the program within the organization by addressing these issues rather than simply whether the program is achieving its goals. Evaluative research that does not use a systems model should note some of these larger organizational issues in the program description.

5. *Program Funding and Cost*
How is the program funded? Is it funded through public, private, state, federal, or local money? How much does it cost? Program costs are a very important accountability issue. As Suchman states: "few programs can be justified at any cost" (1967, p. 146). The economy of social programs demands that we consider the most desirable allocations of money, personnel, and facilities.

Program costs are sometimes difficult to determine, especially if the organization uses its continuing operating budget to fund the particular program. We must know what is included in cost. For example, we include direct costs such as the salaries of the staff providing service, but do we include indirect costs such as the cost of staff benefits? One program administrator might include such costs in a total figure and another might not. Comparative costs must be approached cautiously. For example, should we include capital costs or the building and maintenance of the physical plant?

Economic costs should not be isolated, but considered within the context of social costs and social values. If a particular social issue such as the treatment of AIDS surfaces, the social costs and reduction in the death rate of those with the disease might be valued much more than the public monies needed to provide a particular medical intervention. If the rehabilitation of a drug addict or the self-sufficiency of a family on welfare for 10 years is at stake, economic costs must be viewed within the context of larger social costs.

Cost suggests a whole mode of study in program evaluation, involving efficiency and cost-effectiveness. If we know the cost of a program, it will help put into perspective possible outcomes. How efficient is the intervention proposed? How much success can be achieved at what cost? If the field of human services is to shed its naive "do-gooder" image, costs must be taken more seriously. On the other hand, be wary of the administrator or the researcher who is concerned only with cost. A person who is concerned only with costs, is most likely concerned only with cutting costs.

Most program evaluations concern themselves with the overall cost of the program and who funded it. Sometimes the evaluation may be purely a *cost* study, which examines the cost of the intervention and costs of different forms of intervention. Sometimes cost-benefit is studied, that is, cost in relation to the achievement of certain goals or objectives.

6. *The Client or Consumers Served.*

Who are the people being served by the program? What kinds of problems do they have? What aspects of their lives will be changed? How serious are the problems they might have? Do they appear to be motivated to participate in the program? Does the program rationale or logic suggest that they should be motivated to participate in the program? Are the most obvious forms of access to the program in place? For example, if the program was designed for disabled children and their parents is transportation provided? How will people be selected for the program? How are people referred to the program? Are they simply given the telephone number of the organization and told whom to call, or are they screened? Is there a group of people who have agreed to participate? What eligibility criteria exist? Must the clients pay for service? How will outreach be accomplished?

The more you know about the consumers who are served before the program evaluation is implemented, through agency reports or data from a management information system, the better.

Sampling concepts, which will be discussed later as a method for selecting people to be interviewed for a study, can be used to help describe who is served by the program. The researcher discusses the larger group or *target population* for whom the program was planned and the smaller group or *sample* of those who actually use the program? The people participating in a program will frequently differ from a neighborhood group or some other group of people who are not served by the program.

For example, if you are providing a residence for 45 homeless people in a city, you must consider in what ways your *sample* of 45 people is similar or dissimilar from the *target population* of all the homeless people in the city. If the efforts with these 45 people are successful—they are relocated to permanent housing, gain jobs, and stabilize their situations—it would be useful if you could suggest that the program accomplishes this with the larger population of homeless in the city. In this case, the sample is the 45 people served in the program and the target population is a larger population group not served by this program.

Almost without question, groups of people who are served by a program are an *accidental sample*, which usually does not represent a larger group of people. However, we should use our intuition to determine in what ways the people served might differ from other groups of people. Often we have program eligibility criteria that can help us describe how this group of people might be different from or similar to other population groups. Sometimes programs engage in "creaming," whereby the better-off cases are selected. The sample of people in a program is also affected by the types of agencies that refer people to the program. Program attrition, that is, the number of people who drop out of the program, can also affect who is served. Rates of program attrition can demonstrate that the sample of clients who came in for service can be very different from the clients who actually participate in the program.

How people are selected can be crucial to the success or failure of a particular program. Most notable as a problem in this regard is a classic social work study, *Girls at Vocational High* (Meyer, Borgatta, & Jones, 1965), of predelinquent teenagers who received social work service to help prevent delinquent behavior. One criticism of the study involved the awkward manner in which teenagers were recruited for the service. Staff associated with the school contacted the girls and indicated that they might benefit from social work counseling service. Certainly the initial encounter and the way in which the program is explained to people can be critical in determining program success.

7. *Characteristics of the Staff Providing the Service.*
What are the characteristics of the human service workers providing the service? What are their professional backgrounds? Are they social workers, teachers, therapists, group workers, psychologists? What is their past training relative to the interventions used in this program? Once, a classic study in social casework compared the results of long-term and short-term casework, at a private family counseling agency. The agency had a tradition in long-term casework. The agency needed to hire or retrain workers in short-term work. Who would be selected to do the short-term work, and would they be committed to it? The agency setting definitely interacts with the type of intervention used; it also affects the type of practitioners hired (Reid & Shyne, 1969). Questions such as "What are the professionals' perspectives on the model of intervention being utilized?" are important to ask.

8. *Implementation Issues.*
What are the key bottlenecks or early successes in implementing the program design? How has the program been implemented so far? Do the interventive theories appear to be appropriate? Are people coming for service? Are they the types of clients we expected to come? Has the program developed the proper referral sources from which people can be referred to the program? Is the funding received on time, allowing program to operate on its original timetable? Have the appropriate staff been recruited or did we train staff because they did not have the experience to perform the particular type of service? Has the amount of outreach work been underestimated and has this delayed program implementation? Are there still major disagreements within the agency about the program concept and where the program should be headed in terms of planning?

Concern with implementation issues can help you circumvent problems where you find that the planner says the plan was good, but it was not implemented in the proper way. If issues in implementation are key, the researcher may decide to do an implementation study or a program monitoring study to examine program implementation and program operations. In the next chapter, we will outline how to do these studies.

To write the program description, not every question in every area necessarily needs to be examined before the evaluation proceeds. The above list is meant to be an aid in developing a comprehensive program description. Certainly, the researcher needs to generate as good a program description as possible, before proceeding to the second step of defining the program goals.

NEEDS-ASSESSMENT STUDIES IN PROGRAM EVALUATION

In discussing the description of the program, we have assumed two factors, that the need for the program is clearly established and that the program is operational. If the need for the program is not clearly established, evaluation research can evaluate the need for the program. There also may be times when the program is operational, but the need for the program has never been established clearly. Administrators, staff, or funding bodies may decide that they need to reassess and clarify the need for the program. More planning may be required to determine whether a particular program should be in operation, which interventive methods should be used, and so on. These planning studies are usually called *needs-assessment studies*. Needs-assessment studies are an important part of the field of program evaluation.

As an example, a university may be planning an employee assistance program to help their employees with some of the problems of everyday life in the workplace and at home. In planning the program, a number of programming options for groups of employees might be considered. The program could offer group programs for employees to discuss issues related to the family, such as divorce, single-parenting, caring for an elderly family member, parenting an adolescent child, and so on. Likewise, the program could offer a whole range of groups relating to personal health and wellness, such as weight reduction, stress in the workplace and in homelife, nutrition, exercise, and so on. Or, the program could offer groups that are more directly work-related, such as how to control a difficult employee, how to provide creative supervision of employees, and so forth.

The survey of potential consumers could include the following types of questions to assess which groups the employees thought were more valuable:

Which of the following group programs would you like the employee assistance program to offer? (CHECK ALL THAT APPLY.)

____ Weight Watchers

____ Aerobics Classes

____ Other Exercise

____ Discussions about balancing work and family demands

____ Discussions on care of and resources for aging parents

____ Discussions about topics such as depression

____ Discussions about substance abuse and its effects on families

Which of the following skills-development workshops would you like the employee assistance program to offer or to continue to offer? (CHECK ALL THAT APPLY.)

____ How to chair a meeting

____ Purposes of staff meetings, agendas, frequency of meetings, etc.

____ Discussions on disagreements with supervisors

____ How to communicate work expectations to subordinates

____ How to use a work evaluation to improve your skills

____ How to write clear and concise minutes

____ How to use informal department get-togethers to improve relationships?

Likewise, needs-assessment could be used to explore a number of one-to-one service options that were possible for the program. Employees might use the program for assistance in the use of community resources or for personal counseling. The following planning questions were asked to assess which types of one-to-one service might be offered.

If you had a financial problem, a problem with housing, a problem finding a home-care person for an aged relative, or a problem finding day care for your child, would you contact the university EAP?

____ Yes

____ No

____ Not sure

If not, why not? _____

_____

If you had a personal problem such as being depressed or anxious or a problem in a close relationship, would you come to the university EAP to talk to a staff person there?

____ Yes

____ No

____ Not sure

If not, why not? _____

_____

As part of the planning process, program staff could conduct a needs-assessment study to determine which programming paths to follow. Needs-assessment studies often employ a variety of research techniques. One of the most prevalent techniques is a *survey of potential consumers* to determine which types of services they think would most likely utilize. In this case, all employees could be surveyed to see what types of employee assistance programs they might use. A survey also could be conducted of other university-based employee assistance programs to assess the kinds of services they offer, the interventive methods used, and the types of practice skills needed for such programs.

In addition to surveys, *census reports and population data* are often used to examine the need for a program. In this example, the employee assistance program could review the characteristics of the university population to determine the number of different types of employees and their sociodemographic characteristics to determine the need for particular types of services. For example, how many single parents are there in the population? How many employees have families with young children? How many employees were recently hired and may be experiencing work-adjustment problems?

Census data from the government may be especially valuable for needs-assessment studies. For example, a local community group that wanted to help the poor in their community could use census data to determine the numbers of people living on SSI, AFDC, and so on.

Another methodology that can be used in a needs-assessment study is a *review of the literature.* For example, the university-based employee assistance program could examine the literature on university programs to determine the type of programs that are usually offered and their relative success.

Needs-assessment studies differ from goal-oriented program evaluation in that *client needs* not program goals are being assessed. Evaluative researchers are particularly skillful at carrying out needs-assessment studies because they are more familiar with the research methodology.

In needs-assessment studies, the first two steps differ from the steps in program evaluation. Instead of describing the program, you begin by describing the possible needs that the program could address and the alternative ways the program could meet those needs. Then, rather than defining the program goals, you define possible needs and program options. The third, fourth, fifth, and sixth steps are similar to goal-oriented evaluation. You still must design methodolgy for the study, implement the study and collect the data, analyze the data, and report your findings. If the study employs a survey methodology, the methodology must address sampling issues. You must select a method of data analysis. If you are using census data or other secondary data, your method will be similar to evaluation studies that utililze secondary data as a methodology. If you are conducting a literature review, you will spell out the methodology for selecting literature and qualitatively analyze the trends in the literature.

The logic and the model of needs-assessment studies is outlined in Figure 3.1.

FIGURE 3.1 Logic and model of needs-assessment studies.

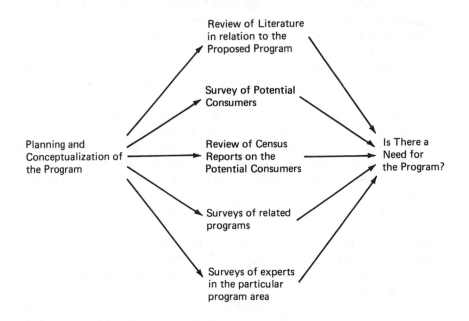

One word of caution about needs-assessment studies. First, social need is a soft concept that involves values about what is defined as a need. The answers provided by needs-assessment studies are often very tentative ones. Surveys that study needs often require that potential consumers put themselves in the hypothetical situation of whether they would seek help with a particular problem. For example, in the employee assistance program, 124 employees said that they were interested in group discussions of how to care for an aging parent, but only 25 employees signed up for the group when it was offered.

Second, need is a complex phenomena that includes needs, resources, the cost of trained personnel and staff, and community attitudes about the types of programs the public is willing to accept. Suchman notes that needs are problems that affect a whole group of people and needs eventually get translated into immediate and ultimate program objectives (Suchman, 1967). Needs-assessment studies contain the seeds for further program evaluations after the program is operational.

Sometimes, rather than conducting a needs-assessment study, it is better to evaluate a small version of the program and people's reactions to it. Implementing a pilot program often gives a better representation of whether there is a real need for the program. All evaluation studies, including those that assess the program in operation or program outcomes, have needs-assessment components. For example, difficulties in operating a program may stem from the lack of need and the achievement of outcomes also could be blocked because there is no need for the program.

SUMMARY OF KEY IDEAS IN THIS CHAPTER

These are the key points you should remember from this chapter:

1. Through the use of the methods of social science, we can achieve better *descriptions* of social phenomena such as social programs. Scientific method may be used for *exploration* and *description* as well as for *prediction*.

2. Describing the program may very well be the most important part of program evaluation. Without an adequate program description, how will we know what worked and what did not work?

3. Social programs change and we need an updated description if we want to do program evaluation.

4. Social programs have both *quantitative* (e.g., the number of training sessions) and *qualitative* (e.g., personal style of the trainer) aspects to them. Comprehensive program descriptions help document the qualitative aspects of programs.

5. Written program descriptions should include the following:

   1. An Overview of the Program and the Program Rationale
   2. The Interventive Methods Used
   3. Key Elements in the Program Field or Context
   4. The Setting Where the Program is Being Conducted
   5. Program Funding and Cost
   6. The Clients or Consumers Served
   7. The Characteristics of the Staff Providing Service
   8. Implementation Issues

6. Needs-assessment studies are an important part of the field of program evaluation. These studies can include surveys of potential consumers, surveys of related programs, surveys of experts in the particular program area, analyses of community or institutional population data, and literature reviews.

EXERCISES FOR THIS CHAPTER

1. Take a written description of a program you know about and try to update the description by addressing the areas mentioned in this chapter.

2. For a program that you know about, describe some aspects of the program that are more qualitative in nature and describe aspects of it that are quantitative.

3. Interview one administrator and one line worker who has direct contact providing service in a program you know about. What areas of agreement do they have about the program and what are their areas of disagreement?

4. For a program you know about, state the program's general rationale and purpose. What more specific goals and objectives can you identify that are related to the program's purpose?

REFERENCES

Babbie, E. (1986). *The practice of social research* (pp. 72–74). Belmont, CA: Wadsworth Publishing Co.

Etzioni, A. (1960). Two approaches to organizational analysis: A critique and a suggestion. *Administrative Science Quarterly*, 5 (2), 257–278.

Meyer, H., Borgatta, E., & Jones, W. (1957). *Girls at vocational high: An experiment in social work intervention.* New York: Russell Sage Foundation.

Reid, W., & Shyne, A. (1969). *Brief and extended casework.* New York: Columbia University Press.

Rossi, P.H., & Freeman, H.E. (1986). *Evaluation: A systematic approach* (pp. 87–92). Beverly Hills, CA: Sage Publications.

Suchman, E.A. (1967). *Evaluative research.* New York: Russell Sage Foundation.

Weiss, C.H. (1972). *Evaluation research: Methods of assessing program effectiveness* (p. 43). Englewood Cliffs, NJ: Prentice-Hall.

4

The Second Step:
Defining the Program Goals

THE IMPORTANCE OF GOALS

As human beings it is useful for us to have goals. You might have the career goal of becoming a human service professional, a social worker, a teacher, a counselor, or a therapist. This is why you are going to school or working in a school, social agency, counseling center, etc. You also have more immediate goals: to get an A in a particular course, to complete all of your assignments for this semester, or to make it to the end of a particularly boring class session, to complete your day at work, to go out to a ball game. Because you are in the human services field, you most likely do not have goals such as buying a BMW car within the next year.

Once my wife and I tried an interesting experiment in which we separately listed our goals for the next five years. The results and the discussion following this exercise led to some interesting interaction. Examining the "we" goals versus the "me" goals on each list was instructive. It is important for us to have goals. Likewise, it is important for programs to have goals. Program goals help establish where the program is headed.

In the last chapter, we learned that the first step of program evaluation is describing and defining the program. We might say, then, that the first research question in program evaluation is "What is the program?" Imbedded in the program concept is the general purpose and rationale of the program and the program goals. Once you know what the program is and what the general purpose of the program is, you can proceed to a more explicit statement of those goals.

Thus the second step in program evaluation is defining the program goals. The second major research questions in program evaluation are: "What are the program goals?" and "Which of those goals do you intend to study?"

WHAT IS A GOAL IN RESEARCH TERMS?

In research, we talk about dependent and independent variables. Dependent variables are things we suspect are the effects and independent variables are things we suspect are causes. An easy way to remember this is that effects are dependent upon causes and so the dependent variable DEPENDS on the independent variable. In the physical sciences, a dependent variable might be a person's blood pressure and an independent variable might be a drug that we suspect reduces a person's high blood pressure.

What type of variables are the goals in evaluation research? The goals are the dependent variables. These are the outcomes, the gains we might hope to see as a result of the program. What are the independent variables for program evaluation? The program itself is certainly the major independent variable in program evaluation. This is what we hope will create some change in the dependent variable or outcome variable.

If a researcher were evaluating an alcoholism program, one of the program goals might be cessation of drinking alcoholic beverages. This would be the dependent variable. One of the program inputs might be the individual therapeutic sessions. One independent variable would then be the number of therapeutic sessions. We hope that the program inputs, the number of individual therapeutic sessions, has a positive effect in eliminating alcoholism in the client population. In a marital counseling program, the rate of marital satisfaction might be a goal or one of the dependent variables. The number of joint therapeutic sessions might be an independent variable that we hope causes the effect.

There are other independent variables, of course, that might cause a change in the dependent variable. The characteristics of the clients given service are a set of independent variables. The type of people served would be another factor that might cause a change in the results of the program. For example, an alcoholism program can be expected to be more successful if the client population does not have a chronic history of alcoholism.

Some parts of the program, are more clearly measurable than others— for example, the frequency of contact with the service provider or a list of the types of services given. Other variables—for example, the philosophies of the different practitioners providing service—are not as easily quantifiable.

A good way to begin formulating the goals of the program is to diagram them under the heading "dependent variables." This is an excellent exercise in problem formulation and in explicating the program goals. You also might make a heading "independent variables" and list the major dependent and independent variables in the program, and this is sometimes a useful way to get a realistic handle on the evaluation. This independent-dependent typology is a good way to organize your research study.

FIGURE 4.1. Major independent and dependent variables in evaluating an alcoholism program.

1. Alcoholism Program

    Independent Variables ⟶ *Dependent Variables*

    Individual therapeutic intervention ⟶ Cessation of drinking alcohol (6 months, 12 months, etc.)

    Client characteristics Chronicity of alcoholism and other client variables ⟶ Individual therapeutic intervention ⟶ Cessation of drinking alcohol (6 mths., 12 mths. etc.)

    Client characteristics Chronicity of alcoholism and other client variables ⟶ Individual therapeutic intervention plus Alcoholics Anonymous meetings ⟶ Cessation of drinking alcohol (6 mths., 12 mths., etc.)

2. Marital Counseling Program

    Independent Variables ⟶ *Dependent Variables*

    Conjoint family therapy Number of sessions Types of sessions Types of interventions ⟶ Marital satisfaction

In Figure 4.1, a diagram of the independent and dependent variables for the evaluation of an alcoholism treatment program is presented. Notice that the evaluative model is stated simply in the first part of the diagram, with therapeutic intervention as the independent variable and the cessation of drinking as the dependent variable. The second part of the diagram introduces client variables as a second type of independent variable. The third part of the diagram adds more independent variables, individual therapeutic intervention plus attendance at Alcoholics Anonymous meetings to the study. The last part diagrams the major independent and dependent variables in an evaluation of a marital counseling program.

One caution, however, about independent and dependent variables. You must realize that the terms cause and effect are used loosely here. Just because you diagram certain things as dependent and independent variables does not automatically make them causes or effects. If, for example, we are studying whether or not alcoholism rate is affected by the number of therapeutic encounters, we also must investigate other factors in the client's life that may be causing the effect. Causal relationships are very difficult to prove in social science research.

PROGRAM GOALS AND PROGRAM OBJECTIVES

As you start listing the goals of the program, you will notice one thing. Some of what you have listed as goals are very broad and others are more specific. For example, let us say you are evaluating a group program in a senior center that hopes to improve socialization among the elderly. To improve socialization could be one of the major program goals and is very broad. There are other goals that are part of improved socialization that are more specific, such as to increase the quantity and quality of the interaction within the group, to increase the social interaction of members outside the group, to increase their interaction with relatives, friends, and neighbors, and to increase their participation in community organizations and programs outside the senior center. These more specific items are the program *objectives* under the more general goal of increased socialization.

A goal is an end or an outcome toward which effort is directed. Program goals are based on values. We value obtaining employment for people, getting them off drugs, improving a person's self concept, and so on. A goal is an ending or terminal value, it is where we *wish* to be. Hopefully, we will find that is more than a wish, and that some progress is made toward the goal. Program goals are broader outcomes we wish to achieve.

Program objectives are more specific outcomes we wish to achieve. Objectives are based upon instrumental values. Objectives tell us "how to" achieve the goals. Specific objectives must be achieved before we can say that the more general goal is achieved.

Program goals and objectives were mentioned when you described the program in the first step of program evaluation. However, in the second step in program evaluation, program goals and objectives need to be stated more specifically.

In the example of the group program in a senior center, the program goal was to increase the socialization of the elderly and prevent social isola-

TABLE 4.1 Program Goals and Objectives for a Program to Increase Socialization for the Elderly

Dependent Variables	
Program Goal:	To increase socialization of the elderly
Program Objectives:	1. To increase seniors' involvement at the Senior Center.
	2. To increase participation in community organizations and groups
	3. To increase social involvement with friends and neighbors.
	4. To increase social activities.

tion. The more specific program objectives might be to increase the seniors' involvement in activities at the center, to increase their involvement in other community groups, to increase their involvement with friends and neighbors, and to increase their social activities. The goals and objectives of this program are diagrammed in Table 4.1. Notice that we are beginning to measure the concept of socialization by looking at the particular objectives.

Specifying the objectives in the above way is the beginning step in *operationalizing* these objectives, that is, describing them in a way that allows them to be measured. This will be completed in the third step, when the researcher determines what data collection strategy or strategies will be needed and what questions will be asked that *operationalize* the program goals and objectives. In our example above, the researcher might simply interview the seniors before and after the group program and ask them questions about the frequency and self-perceived quality of their interactions with family, neighbors, and friends and about their participation in other community organizations. In this case, operationalization will culminate in the development of a series of questions to measure the goal of increased socialization.

Some objectives are *process objectives* and are more closely related to the means to achieve the goals. For example, in the senior program, the objective might be to increase the interaction of the seniors within the group itself, thereby achieving the program goal of increased socialization. The role of such a process objective is diagrammed in Table 4.2. Detailing the objectives in this way can give you more specific information about *how* the intervention is supposed to work.

TABLE 4.2 Process Objective and Program Goal for Program to Increase Socialization of the Elderly

Process Objectives:	Program goal and objectives
Increased interaction of the seniors within the group program	Objectives: 1. Increased involvement of seniors at the center. 2. Increased participation in community groups. 3. Increased social interaction with friends and neighbors. 4. Increase in social activities.

A WORD OF CAUTION ABOUT PROGRAM GOALS

The evaluator needs to be cautious about program goals. Goals are sometimes too broad and too vague to be useful for research purposes. For example, the goal of a day treatment program for mentally disabled homeless women is "to create a therapeutic environment that will enable mentally disabled homeless women to develop to the best of their own abilities so they can lead productive lives." The program hopes to do this through dance therapy, visual arts, social work intervention, job readiness skills, life skills groups, and a housing readiness program. Clearly, the program goal as stated is too broad and vague to be useful. However, we could more easily study program objectives such as the perceptions of women about whether the center provides a supportive atmosphere. Or, we could study the life skills groups to determine which life skills were taught successfully.

Goals are sometimes pious platitudes about the program. For example, the goals of a foster care program might be to return children home to their biological parents. This often is not possible, however, because the parent is seriously incapacitated or does not have the resources to maintain the primary household. Sometimes goals are totally unrealistic, for example, you might have agreed to find jobs for 200 unemployed youth by September 30 in order to obtain funding from a particular source.

Program goals or objectives can also lack substance. For example, the goal of a counseling service to provide three counseling sessions and the goal of a training session to provide 12 training sessions illustrate goals that are more process objectives. If in these cases, more substantial goals are not studied, you are engaging in administrative monitoring, not goal-oriented evaluation research.

Program goals can be purely ritualistic and sometimes should not be taken seriously. For example, a state funding source says that your agency should conduct AIDS training, but the agency does not have a great commitment to that type of programming. Or, the funding source says you should develop programs for the homeless, but the agency is not equipped for these types of programs.

Obtaining the official list of the goals of the program or creating that list is one of the practice tasks of the evaluator. If too many of the goals are vague, pious platitudes about the program, or unrealistic and un-achieveable, the researcher should develop an *evaluability assessment* of the program to determine to what extent one can evaluate the program (Rossi & Freeman, 1989). If the program administrator is convinced that these vague, unrealistic, or ritualistic goals are the only ones that people want to study, the researcher might determine that the evaluation cannot be conducted at this point in time. If the program administrator is willing to change some of the goals or add more realistic goals, the assessment may conclude that the research can continue. In either case, the function of the evaluability assessment is to address the nature of program goals and to develop more specific, realistic goals.

The researcher is *pro-active* in relation to the goals. The researcher *finds* the goals and may even *create* some of the goals and objectives. This is another task in the *practice* of evaluation research.

If you have a choice, studying objectives rather than goals is preferable for research purposes, because objectives are more specific and measurable. Studying program objectives gives us a solid base from which we can study the more general program goals. Objectives themselves help us to be more specific about program goals.

You should realize that we may achieve some of the program objectives but we may not achieve the program goals. For example, you might find that you have increased the senior citizens' activities at the center, but there was no change in their involvement with friends and neighbors. You may find that the program has increased socialization in one area but decreased socialization in another area. In that case you would be uncertain about whether the major goal of increased socialization was achieved.

In addition, you may achieve all of the objectives of the program, but still not achieve the program goals. For example, the goal of a public health nursing program might be to keep children healthy. The particular objec-tives might be to give the children inoculations, to see they get medical exams, and to ensure that they are visited regularly by school nurses. You may achieve all of these objectives, but the children may still get sick and their attendance at school may remain the same as before they participated in the program. The objectives were achieved but the goals were not.

If we study programs at the level of *program objectives*, the more likely we are to find that simple interventions work. For example, getting the school bus driver to assist a mildly disabled child on and off the bus often helps achieve the objective of increasing the child's school attendance. Or, buying a washing machine for a low-income family with a developmentally disabled child will help achieve the objective of reducing the burden and the stress on the parent. With the washing machine in the home, the parent does not have to negotiate taking three children, one of whom is developmentally disabled, to the local laundromat.

In program management there are certain approaches that are based upon rational statements of program goals and objectives. The PERT model thoroughly explores comprehensive program goals and their relations to program objectives. The model spells out program activities and examines the relation between activities and objectives. "Management by objective" approaches to administration also comprehensively examine program goals and objectives (Suchman, 1967).

TYPES OF GOALS AND OBJECTIVES

Program goals and objectives are the dependent variables in program evaluation. There are a number of different typologies that help us conceptualize the program goals. Thinking about these goal typologies is a good method to determine the program goals and objectives and to determine the focus of the program evaluation.

Proximate Goals and Ultimate Goals

There are *proximate goals and ultimate goals*. Proximate goals are more immediate, short-term or formative goals. Proximate goals look more like objectives than goals. Proximate goals are often program *process objectives*. For example, in a hospital treatment program for schizophrenics, providing a supportive atmosphere or making some therapeutic connection to the patients might be proximate goals. Ultimate goals are more substantial changes with longer-term effects. An ultimate goal for the schizophrenic treatment program might be a decrease in the hospitalization rate among the group of patients. Ultimate goals include changes in knowledge, attitude, or behavior; changes in people's adjustment or psychological state; obtaining employment; reduction in the rate of substance abuse; reduction of family violence; and an increase in independent living for mentally ill populations.

The proximate–ultimate typology suggests major differences in approach to program evaluation. Human service professionals are sometimes ridiculed for being too concerned with proximate goals. However, in the above example you can see that connecting with a schizophrenic client may be a much more realistic goal than reducing further hospitalizations. If it can be shown that the program did this, at the least we have shown some results, although it failed in the ultimate goal of preventing further hospitalizations. The program also has an advantage over programs that might not be able to create this sense of connectedness.

Other proximate, short-range goals might be to provide a program that people attend and find useful; to provide a program that has a positive, supportive atmosphere; to provide a program that people like; or to provide a program where people interact well with professionals providing service. "Wait," you say, "could such things possibly be goals worth studying?" All I need do is remind you about programs you may have attended or been involved in where even these kinds of goals were not achieved. Many programs that are funded for thousands, even millions of dollars, often could not have passed the test of achieving these proximate goals.

Kogan and Shyne discuss *tender-hearted and tough-minded* approaches to program evaluation (Kogan & Shyne, 1966). Focusing on formative program goals is a more tender-hearted approach, while focusing on ultimate goals is a more tough-minded approach. More tender-hearted approaches often are more valuable for uncovering the logic and process of the intervention and initial program experiences. Proximate goals can be useful in their own right, even if they are not necessarily the goals that accountability agencies are looking for. It is often the function of the *evaluator-practitioner* to give people an appreciation for more formative, tender-hearted approaches. Program administrators who take a tender-hearted approach to programs should be admired. For example, in developing a university-based employee assistance program, the university president advanced the notion that the program was for employees to seek help with any of their problems, and the president allowed the program to develop so that employees could use it for discussion of personal problems or help with consumer, legal, or social problems. An alternate model of forcing employees to use the service for substance abuse problems was discarded. The president's tender-hearted approach also carried over to the evaluation. The program was given a chance to develop, and formative goals and monitoring data—such as the number of employees using the program—were used in the early years as indicators of the success of the program, before goal-oriented evaluation was developed.

The ideas of proximate versus ultimate goals and tender-hearted versus tough-minded approaches run parallel to another major perspective in evaluation research—*formative versus summative* approaches to program evaluation. The formative-summative perspective was first presented by Scriven (1967). He recognized that there were formative and summative *uses* for evaluative research. Formative uses focus on feedback of short-range program findings to improve the program as it continues. Summative uses focus on whether the program should continue by studying its effectiveness in achieving its ultimate goals. Summative approaches emphasize ultimate goals.

The proximate-ultimate typology should be viewed as a continuum, with activities such as creating a supportive atmosphere or providing a service for a group of people on the proximate side of the continuum and activities such as helping the client end drug or alcohol abuse or obtain steady employment on the ultimate side of the continuum. In formulating a research plan for evaluation research, it is often a helpful method to sketch possible goals on the proximate-ultimate continuum.

The proximate-ultimate typology introduces the notion that in any particular program there are *multiple* goals. Usually each of these goals may have a number of subgoals and objectives. If we find that there are just too many goals to study, we must *partialize* the goals and conduct research on only some of the goals. For example, if we conduct a program evaluation by interviewing people at the program's completion, and it is only possible to conduct one half-hour interview, obviously we would be limited in asking questions about the program. Some of the goals could not be studied if the evaluation had to occur in only one half-hour interview. Hopefully, the researcher would find ways to conduct another interview so as to study more of the program's goals.

Program Goals and Practice Goals

In particular, if we are evaluating a clinical or treatment program, we should introduce the concepts of *program goals* and *practice goals*. In clinical research, it is possible to do some research on individual case goals or practice objectives. For example, in a marital counseling program, trying to help a husband be less abusive to his wife might be a case goal. We could do clinical research on whether this one goal was achieved in this particular case or in a group of cases. However, if we were evaluating the whole counseling program, this might not be a goal that applies to all cases. A goal such as improving marital relations or overall personal satisfaction might be more acceptable program goals because these goals fit every case.

In initiating program evaluation, the practice goal-program goal typology is useful because often in developing program goals we can start with some individual case goals. If these goals apply to all cases in the program they might become useful program goals to study.

If the researcher is more interested in studying individual case goals at the micro level, there are two bodies of knowledge that would help. One methodology, which emphasizes measuring individual case goals, is called GAS or Goal Attainment Scaling (Kiresuk & Sherman, 1968). This methodology originated in the community mental health field. In goal attainment scaling, individual case goals are rated and combined through a complex scoring procedure. A second methodology for studying achievement of goals in individual cases is the $N = 1$ case study. The $N = 1$ case study is an experimental approach in which changes in the achievement of case objectives are studied (Jayaratne & Levy, 1979). For example, in one case, you might measure the number of marital conflicts at the beginning of service and then at a later time to determine if any reductions occurred in the frequency of marital conflicts.

Unanticipated Goals

Among the many ways to view goals, we should be aware of the concept of *unanticipated goals* or *serendipitous outcomes*. At every point along the way, the researcher should be aware of possible outcomes that were not originally conceived when the evaluation study was planned and conducted. For example, a single-parent family program was supposed to develop support groups of single parents throughout New York City. The groups were designed to cut down on the isolation of single parents and help them solve similar problems such as child care, initiating career plans, and so on. One of the most positive parts of the program, however, was incidental to the overall program. The program was especially successful in drawing the media's attention to the situation of single parents. This was an unanticipated outcome for the program evaluators. However, in their final report, the evaluators were able to describe the project's extensive media efforts and report it as an outcome that seemed to be achieved. There are no scientific principles violated in reporting this although the major thrust of the evaluation plan had been to document the group program. In the practice of program evaluation, the researcher needs to be attentive to these emerging unanticipated goals.

The better the program evaluation is planned and the more comprehensive the formulation of program objectives, the fewer unanticipated consequences the researcher should find. If the *researcher-practitioner*, in describing the program, observes the program in operation, keeps brainstorming, and keeps talking to people about the program, he or she will be uncovering new goals that can be studied *before* initiating the evaluation.

Even after the researcher starts the evaluation and has determined a finite set of program goals for evaluation, he or she can include in the evaluation strategy formative tactics. For example, if you are designing an interview with people who received service from the program, ask them open-ended questions such as, "What did you get out of this program?" to uncover possible benefits you failed to consider initially. After the study begins, the researcher should be sensitive to possible unanticipated goals and continue to observe the program informally and continue to talk to people about the program. Unanticipated goals can become new goals of the program and can be included in future evaluations. One of the values of program evaluation is that it makes explicit the program's goals and objectives that were *unanticipated* when the program was planned and implemented.

Changes in Knowledge, Attitude, Skills, and Behavior

Generically, social programs are often designed to bring about changes in knowledge, attitude, skills, and behavior. This is another way to conceptualize the program goals. Later, when we discuss design, we will mention pre-and post-studies that test program participants before and after the program and are effective ways for studying change. In a more formative evaluation, you might interview people after the program to determine what they thought about the program and ask them if they thought there were changes in knowledge, attitude, skills, or behavior; which sessions in the program seemed to affect them more relative to possible changes; and if the manner in which the material was presented might have resulted in changes.

When we think about change in knowledge, we often think of educational programs. That is, people attend classes, the researcher determines if they know certain material before the class starts, and then retests them at the end of the semester to ascertain any gains in their knowledge.

The purpose of many social programs is to give clients or consumer more knowledge. Sometimes the goal is to make people more knowledgeable about a certain social problem. For example, a group program might be initiated to increase drug addicts' knowledge about the danger of AIDS. Sometimes the goal might be to increase people's knowledge about community resources. For example, one of the goals of a support group for people who care for their elderly relatives at home could be to increase the person's knowledge about social services and entitlements. If the relatives' knowledge about home care, SSI, Medicaid, and senior citizen programs is increased there may be a greater possibility that the relatives will use that particular social service.

Change in knowledge is almost always a goal in training programs for new staff in the human service setting. For example, we might want to give social workers knowledge about a new theory of child development that they can apply to their work. Likewise, we may train child welfare workers to use a family approach in foster care and to pay more attention to the biological parent of a child in foster care.

While it seems straightforward to judge if individuals have increased their level of knowledge, it is sometimes hard to show cause and effect. For example, people are often affected by the test-taking situation itself—referred to as the *testing effect*. If people are given the test before the program begins, they may find the answers to questions they did not know on their own, and the increase in knowledge may not be attributable to their training or teaching alone. However, for program purposes, we know that knowledge was increased, even if the program did not *directly* cause the increase. Also, gaining knowledge does not necessarily mean the person will *use* that knowledge. So, in a typical program where we study changes in knowledge, we also may want to study changes in behavior.

Attitudes, values, and *belief systems* is another major conceptual arena to seek change in individuals. For example, we might have a training program in which we try to change social workers' attitudes toward foster parents. Or, we could research a program designed to change people's attitudes toward developmentally disabled children. We might evaluate a delinquency prevention program that hopes to help delinquent children take on some of the attitudes of nondelinquent children. Luckily, psychologists and psychometricians have spent many hours developing and refining scales that can measure a variety of attitudes and beliefs. Since our attitudes, values, and belief systems take a lifetime to develop, however, attitude change, and especially changes in values and belief systems, may be difficult to achieve given the usual level of intervention in educational and social programs.

An increase in *skills* is another major domain to seek changes in individuals. Prevocational, vocational, and job-training programs that teach job-specific skills are typical examples. The evaluation of a person's ability to perform a certain job task at the end of the program is another type of assessment that specialists perform in the job-development field. The researchers may use standard measures to assess the learning of job tasks or they can develop original measures of outcome.

Professional skill development is another type of increase in skill. We might assess a program in which social workers are supposed to learn skills in family interaction techniques or in group work. Professional skill may be an especially complex area to study, because it includes the skills themselves as well as the process of incorporating the knowledge and values upon which the profession is based.

Behavior is a final arena in which to seek change in individuals. Changes in behavior are frequently the easiest to define but the most difficult to achieve. For example, we might evaluate a program that assists a group in making greater use of community resources. Or, we might evaluate a program that encourages senior citizens to engage in more social activities. Decreased drug use, fewer marital arguments, a reduction in delinquent activities, are areas in which social programs often seek change.

One of the difficulties in measuring behavior change is that people are more likely to report socially desirable and acceptable behavior, and self-reports of behavior change may be especially unreliable. In this case, the person's own report should be supplemented with outside data and formal records—court reports, school records, and professional reports or interviews with social workers, psychologists, and so forth. Using an additional data source increases the credibility or reliability of the data. Investigating one result by using two data sources is termed *triangulation* (Patton, 1988).

Those programs that use techniques of behavior modification have an obvious advantage in this area. In fact, the intervention itself may be primarily aimed at changing a very specific behavior. Such programs might have a headstart in producing specific behavior change, and the researcher needs to note this.

As far as changes in knowledge, attitude, skill, and behavior are concerned, we should not necessarily expect changes in all of these goal areas. One typical example involves programs where some attitude change occurs, but no change occurs in behavior. Typically, program evaluation finds that some goals are achieved while others are not. That is the true value of program evaluation. It is very helpful to provide feedback about goals that are achieved to those involved in the program and to those who fund the program. Feedback about unachieved goals can be used to help change a program so that it can become more succesful—no matter how painful this news may be.

Often no norms exist of how much change to expect in a particular program. In assessing change, *time* is a very important variable. How long will it take for substantial change to take place? For how long will these changes last after the program's end? Will there be no change initially, but will change occur some time after a person's participation in the program? The latter is called the "sleeper effect" (Weiss, 1972). In spite of the many difficulties in establishing these effects, change in knowledge, attitude, skills, and behavior will *always* be critical goals in evaluation research.

RELIABILITY AND VALIDITY IN THE MEASUREMENT OF PROGRAM GOALS

After determining the goals of the program, we must *operationalize* them. Operationalization simply means that we find ways to make program goals and objectives measurable. A comprehensive case example of how to operationalize a simple training program is presented at the end of this chapter. For now, let us say that a major goal of a program you are studying is to increase the self-esteem of a group of people. Operationalizing this goal means that we must define self-esteem, breaking it into aspects or components that can be measured, for example, through questionnaire items.

In operationalizing the definition of any program goal, there are two criteria that must be kept in mind: reliability and validity. These are two measurement issues that social scientists struggle with. Notice I said *struggle*. Issues of reliability and validity are never completely resolved, except perhaps in research heaven. One needs only to mention the ongoing debates about how to measure intelligence or how to assess competency through civil service tests or professional accrediting exams, to realize this fact.

In reality, issues of reliability and validity often receive less attention in evaluation research than in basic research on families and individuals. Basic measurement issues are sometimes overlooked in program evaluation so as to obtain initial data on the program's progress.

Reliability means the *strength* or *consistency* of the process by which you collect your data on the program and of the questions and items you ask in your data collection instrument or questionnaire. Most students remember reliability from the notion of *test-retest*. For example, a psychometrician might develop a series of 10 checklist questions to measure self-esteem. If these questions are reliable in measuring self-esteem, the self-esteem scores of a large group of people today would be similar to their scores ten weeks from today. In other words, the scores show some consistency in measuring a state of self-esteem in people. Furthermore, if each of these 10 items measure self-esteem on an index or scale, each item on the scale should be related to the total score on self-esteem and the items should be related to one another.

For example, Rosenberg (1965) developed 10 items to measure the concept of self-esteem. People were asked to check "Strongly Agree," "Agree," "Disagree," or "Strongly Disagree" on 10 separate questionnaire items. This type of scale is called a Likert scale. It includes the following items: "I feel I'm a person of worth, at least on an equal plane with others," "I feel I have a number of good qualities"; "I am able to do things as well as other people"; and so on. Rosenberg found that a person's score on each item is related to his or her score on other items. For example, if you tend to agree you are a person of worth, you also are likely to agree you have a number of good qualities. Furthermore, there will be a relationship between your answer on each item and your total self-esteem score.

One of the simplest, yet most important notions about reliability is what I call *common sense reliability*, or the *reliability of the measurement process* itself. If, for example, in an interview or questionnaire, questions are unclear or are phrased in professional jargon, there will be no stability or consistency to the measurement process. For example, if you ask a person: "Did countertransference get in the way of your counseling?" they might not know what you are asking. Even if they are familiar with these complex concepts, their notions of what they are might vary so much that there would be no reliability or consistency of response. Therefore, researchers need to generate a series of questions that are clear and that measure the concept of countertransference. *Pretesting* a questionnaire or instrument by administering it to a few people before you begin your study is one of the best ways to avoid this type of reliability problem.

Similarly, if we asked a parent, "Is your developmentally disabled child having a problem gaining *access* to services?" you would not get a consistent or reliable response because while some people might know what you mean by access, others would not. A person might say, "No, I am not having a problem with access to services." Yet, if you asked a simple question that provides a clear operational definition of access such as, "Does your child have any difficulty with transportation to the health clinic?" the parent might respond, "Yes!!" These problems of the lack of commonsense reliability in the measurement process can usually be resolved by pretesting your questionnaire. In this way, you can change or remove questions that might cause people confusion.

The second major measurement issue is validity. Validity is defined as the degree to which you are measuring the *concept* you wish to measure. A good deal of validity has some subjectivity written into it. For example, *face validity* means that "on the face of it" your 10 items appear to measure a concept, e.g., self-esteem. In evaluation research, we are more concerned with this first type of validity than with the other types. How well are the questions you ask people measuring the goals of the program "on the face of it"? For example, if one of the proximate goals of the program is to provide a supportive atmosphere to people given service, you should ask questions that will tell you whether this happened.

A more sophisticated notion of validity is *construct* validity. Construct validity denotes the degree to which the questions or items in your data collection instrument measure a theoretical concept. If there are sophisticated concepts in the goals of the program you are evaluating—for example, the goals are to increase marital satisfaction or to increase self-esteem—construct validity would be an issue. Let us say your concept of self-esteem is based on the work of Alfred Adler. You must therefore consider how well your instrument reflects his theoretical framework and his theory about self-esteem. This measurement is somewhat less subjective than face validity because you are comparing your instrument to the outside criteria of Adler's theory. However, as you can see, a judgment process is involved. You may decide that a particular item is an essential part of Adler's theory, while an expert on Adler may say it is not. Also, your method may be viewed with suspicion if you rely solely on Adler's theory, because another researcher may posit that Adler's concept of self-esteem is not mainstream thinking.

A more severe test of validity is *empirical* validity, in which you correlate your measure to an external criteria. For example, if your study measures individuals' self-esteem, their score on the self-esteem scale should be related to factors such as a scale that measures how well they are integrated into their communities. As another example, if you are studying the concept of job satisfaction in a social agency, job satisfaction should be related to external criteria such as the number of unexplained absences from work.

As indicated before, many psychometricians and researchers have spent their lives studying particular concepts and assessing their reliability and validity. We would do well to consult their work in the literature before we start measuring profound concepts such as self-esteem, intelligence, or marital satisfaction, stress, and so on. For example, in a British study where the goal was to relieve stress on parents caring for severely disabled children, the Malaise Scale, a scale of emotional stress, was used to determine if the parents had reduced stress (Bradshaw, 1980). The scale was found to have good reliability and some validity. It included items such as difficulty in sleeping, backaches, health worries, and general irritability. The Malaise scale of emotional stress clearly fit the goals of this program.

Oftentimes, however, you may encounter a very specialized training program whose goal is to provide knowledge about how to refer a client to psychiatric resources. There are probably no standardized instruments to measure this program goal, and you will need to generate some questions yourself that will test whether this knowledge was taught by the program staff. Also, it is a good rule of thumb in evaluation research to include some standard measure of complex concepts and some questions of your own to measure the wide areas where the program was effective.

PROGRAM MONITORING—PART OF THE FIELD OF PROGRAM EVALUATION

Sometimes it is more realistic for you to study program *operations* rather than program goals. Basic information about the program may be required. You spend less time measuring goals and more time answering basic questions such as, "How many clients are in the program?" "What problems brought them in for service?" "What are the sociodemographic characteristics of those in the program?" "What is the intervention?" "Does the intervention 'seem' to be working?" "How do clients perceive the program?" and "Are clients relating in a positive way to service providers?"

Program monitoring is useful in providing basic information for purposes of program accountability. Moreover, a simple rationale exists for doing program monitoring studies. If no one is coming to the program, if clients do not like the program, or if the program has tremendous operational problems, how can the program achieve its goals? Program monitoring addresses these issues.

There are certain characteristics of program-monitoring studies. First, you are asking research questions that are more simple and straightforward than in goal-oriented program evaluation. What is the service? Who are the clients? Who are the workers? Second, program monitoring usually employs a less formal research methodology. Usually you conduct a review of currently existing program data to determine the kind of service is being provided or conduct feedback interviews with a small sample of clients or workers on their views regarding service. Third, you analyze basic facts about the program such as, Who are the clients? How many times do they come for service? What are their perceptions of the program? Fourth, the results should be more easily fedback into the program for program planning purposes. For example, you can use the results to modify the course of the program in midstream by recruiting more clients or a different client population for the program, by using staff differently, or by providing them with more in-service training or more supervision.

Sometimes a study is clearly a program-monitoring study. If you use management information system data or other data on program operations in an initial attempt to monitor the program, you are doing program monitoring. For example, in a university-based employee assistance program that provides counseling and referral services to university employees, you might use data from a management information system to determine: How many clients are seen? Why do they come to the program? What problems would they like to resolve? What are the characteristics in terms of race, ethnicity, sex, age? Use of such data would answer important questions such as: Who uses the program more often, faculty, administrators, or secretarial staff? Do they use the program for information about day care, nursing home placement for an elderly adult, counseling for depression, marital counseling, or help with a substance abuse problem in the family? An example of the type of data collected in a management information system is provided in Appendix B.

Here are two more examples of "pure" program-monitoring studies. If you conduct a cost-accounting study on the costs of particular program interventions, you are doing program monitoring. Likewise, if you conduct telephone interviews with a small sample of clients in the program and ask them what parts of the program they found satisfying, you are doing program monitoring.

In monitoring studies, you also can determine if the policies and philosophies of the program are being implemented. For example, the employee assistance program might want to accept only self-referrals and not employees who are referred by supervisors for substance abuse problems. By examining data on how employees learned of the program, we can monitor whether implementation adhered to the program's philosophy. In any program, monitoring which groups from a particular community use the program provides extremely useful information. Often these are the simple questions that need to be answered about programs before we can go on to study whether or not the program is achieving its goals. For example, you cannot expect the objective to be achieved if little or no service is given.

Usually there is a tremendous overlap between goal-oriented evaluation as defined in this book and program monitoring. Many studies fall somewhere between monitoring studies and goal-oriented evaluation studies. For example, evaluators assessed a program to help families caring for a frail elderly relative in the community (Frankfather, Smith, & Caro, 1981). The program provided home care and social work counseling services to the elderly persons and their families. The evaluation study was clearly a goal-oriented evaluation. The evaluators wanted to see if these services helped maintain the elderly person in the community and prevent nursing home placement. Part of the study also included telephone interviews with a family member to determine if there were any problems implementing the service and which parts of the program seemed beneficial from the family member's perspective. This second part of the evaluation is similar to a monitoring study.

Earlier, we defined program objectives as more specific outcomes that are related to instrumental values of "how to" achieve the goals. When a study emphasizes concrete program objectives related to specific program processes, the study looks more like monitoring and less like goal-oriented program evaluation. Also, when we looked at typologies of goals and objectives we noted that some objectives are formative objectives and were more related to program processes than to program goals and objectives. At other times, we study ultimate goals and are obviously doing goal-oriented evaluation.

Here are two examples of studies that could be either monitoring or goal-oriented evaluation. For example, we might have a program whose objective is to provide 50 homeless families with a safe, secure place to live. By monitoring this program, we find that in fact we have achieved this objective. The program also may have ultimate goals, such as to assist the homeless to find jobs and help make them become more self-sufficient. If you studied only the first objective of providing 50 homeless families with housing, the study probably would be more accurately classified as a program-monitored study. If you also studied its ultimate goals, employment and self-sufficiency, the evaluation would be more accurately classified as goal-oriented program evaluation.

Another example might be a program that refers 50 poor families with disabled children to SSI to receive supplemental income assistance and Medicaid-sponsored home care to help them with the care of the child. This study could be a monitoring study if we only studied whether the 50 families became eligible for SSI and home care. It would be goal-oriented evaluation if we went further and studied the effects of increased income on the family or the effects of the home care in reducing stress on the family.

As a rule, program monitoring is a very useful part of program evaluation and more monitoring studies should be done. Studies emphasizing program monitoring over more substantive issues in relation to goals can be thought of as a "no-frills approach" to program evaluation.

A CASE EXAMPLE: EVALUATION OF A TRAINING PROGRAM IN CHILD WELFARE

The critical problem that has plagued the foster care system for many years is that once children are placed from their own homes into a foster home, the child has little chance of returning home. Research indicates that after six months in care in a foster home, the chances of a child returning home are greatly reduced. The child remains in foster care and very little work is done to reunite the biological family unit. As a result, the child welfare field recognized that more work had to be done with biological parents if there was ever a possibility of reuniting the family. Furthermore, *permanent plans* were needed for the majority of children in foster care, whether this meant reuniting the family unit or terminating parental rights so that the child could be adopted by another family. Federal and state officials wanted to ensure that children would no longer remain in foster care year after year without substantial and realistic planning for their future.

National and state legislation was launched to correct this problem of "drift" in foster care. One outcome of this legislation was called the "service review conference" in foster care. Every three months the biological parent of the child in foster care, the child, and the foster parent met under the direction of the social worker holding the major responsibility for the family. Social workers and other professionals involved in providing services to the family also were involved in these conferences. All were required to set goals for the biological parent and the child. The social workers were told to lead these conferences, but had little knowledge of how the conferences were supposed to work.

To assist these social workers in their new roles at the conferences, a special training program was developed. A formal evaluation component was part of the training. The researcher's job was to translate the goals of the training into easily measured components—the process of operationalization. Goals were translated into questions and items in questionnaires. The questions reflected the goals of the program so as to determine whether the program achieved its goals.

After the researcher described the training and how it would operate (as outlined in the previous chapter), a number of goals were defined for the training program. Similar to the goal types mentioned at the beginning of this chapter, there were *multiple goals*. Furthermore, the goals ranged on a continuum from *proximate goals* to *ultimate goals*.

The researcher detailed a variety of program objectives. The initial goals looked more like proximate objectives and the latter ones looked more like ultimate objectives. The goals were as follows:

PROXIMATE GOALS

1. To provide useful training.
2. To teach topics that the social workers found useful.
3. To change the social workers' thinking about the role of review conferences.
4. To change the social workers' behavior regarding preparation for a review conference.

ULTIMATE GOALS

5. To change social workers' attitudes about biological parents and make them more responsive to the situation of biological parents and others involved in the conferences.
6. To change social workers' more general attitudes about the value of conferences.
7. To change social workers' attitudes about foster care in general.

In the category of proximate goals, one purpose of the training was to provide a useful training experience that would help the social workers in leading the conferences. This goal of "providing useful training" was operationalized in the following way. At the conclusion of the training, the social workers were asked an open-ended question about whether they regarded the training as useful and *why* they regarded the training as useful or not useful. The social workers also were asked their opinions about the strengths and weaknesses of the training so as to identify both positive and negative aspects of the training. The social workers were asked the following questions at the completion of the training:

1A. At the conclusion of the training, did you regard it as a useful experience?

1B. Why?
2.   What did you think were the major strengths of this training program?
3.   What did you think were the major weaknesses of this training program?

While many would criticize this type of data for being too subjective, more is known about the success of training programs that have this type of feedback than those that do not obtain this type of feedback. Moreover, the workers appreciated being treated as fellow professionals who could use their expertise to comment on the value of the training in an open-ended manner, and those who planned the training used the feedback to change aspects of the program that were found to be unhelpful.

In developing questionnaries, researchers often use what is referred to as a *funneling technique*, in which you proceed from asking general and open-ended questions such as those above, to more specific, close-ended questions, rating, and checklists.

The second objective, "to teach topics that the social workers found useful" was operationalized with a checklist of specific topics covered in the training, and workers were asked to rate whether each topic was "very useful," "somewhat useful," or "not useful" to them in their leading of the conferences. The following is the checklist that further operationalized the goal of "providing useful training":

4. Below is a list of the material covered in the training sessions. We are interested in which of the material was especially useful or not useful to you:

Topic	Very useful	Somewhat useful	Not useful
A. Discussion of the positives and negatives of Service Review Conferences.	___	___	___
B. How to prepare for a Conference.	___	___	___
C. How to handle conflict and confrontation (e.g., between child and natural mother, between foster mother and natural mother, etc.)	___	___	___

Comments _____
         _____
         _____

In the final questionnaire, the workers rated 10 major topics in the training. For those who think such data are not helpful, it should be pointed out that results from the above checklist did indicate that certain topics were valued over others. This information gave program planners useful feedback on what seemed to work.

Proximate goals, such as providing training that is useful to these social workers, were complemented by ultimate goals. The training program intended to have an effect on change in attitude. It was hoped that the training would make the social workers more positive about the value of the conferences. Attitude scales were developed, which operationalized the trainees' attitudes about service review conferences. Questions such as the following were administered to the social workers before and after the training:

   5. How valuable do you think review conferences with biological parents present really are?
      _ Extremely valuable _ Valuable _ Not valuable _ Unsure

In addition to attitudes about the service review conferences, one of the goals of the program was to change worker attitudes toward biological parents of the children in foster care. It was hoped that teaching about the conferences would make workers more receptive to the idea of working with biological parents. The following represent some of the close-ended, Likert-scale items asked to determine worker attitudes toward biological parents:

	Strongly agree	Agree	Disagree	Strongly disagree
1. Biological parents are generally responsible people, but they do not have enough financial and social resources to fulfill their roles as parents.	____	____	____	____
2. Most biological parents want their children home.	____	____	____	____

Two other goals of the training included change in attitudes about
foster care in general and about the ability of the foster care system to
achieve the goals of returning children to their biological parents. The
following were the types of items that operationalized attitudes
toward foster care:

	Strongly agree	Agree	Disagree	Strongly disagree
1. Overall the child welfare field was better off before the recent focus on permanency planning.	___	___	___	___
2. The child welfare field today favors the biological parent more than it should.	___	___	___	___

Attitude measures in all these areas were developed and administered before and after the training to see if there was improvement in these attitudes.

The training program also sought to change the workers' skill. In
a more comprehensive research study it may have been possible to observe the performance of social workers at these conferences to determine if there was an improvement in skill at the end of the training.
For the purposes of this study, workers were given examples of conferences before and after the training and asked how they would proceed. Their answers before the training were compared to their
answers at the completion of training to determine if there was an
increase in skill. Workers were also given a checklist of which skills they
thought were important in conducting conferences, so as to determine
if they were more sensitive to the skills involved after the training.

Skill in this instance also overlapped with behavior at the conferences. Other behaviors also were compared. For example, workers
were asked how long it took them to prepare for a conference. It was
assumed that their estimates of the amount of preparation required for
conferences would have increased by the end of training.

These were the major conceptual goals studied in this particular
evaluation. What were the results? How did the training turn out?
Interestingly enough, the training was very well received. So that the
goal of providing useful training was achieved. The training also

helped develop worker skill at conferences. They reported spending more time on planning the conferences and their attitudes improved toward the conferences. However, their attitudes did not improve toward biological parents and foster care. One of the reasons for this was most likely one of the *unanticipated consequences* found in a number of the responses to an open-ended question. In many ways, the workers wrote, the training demonstrated the paradoxes of foster care. They discussed cases in which the biological parent, alcoholic or seriously disturbed, sought help in returning the child home, but would fail to follow through. Some workers said that they were more realistic about the changes they could expect from parents, because training focused upon documenting change in the parent from one service review conference to the next.

SUMMARY OF KEY IDEAS IN THIS CHAPTER

1. The second major step in program evaluation is defining the program goals and objectives. Program objectives must be succinctly defined so that we can measure them and ask people questions that are related to the goals of the program and questions that will inform us whether the goals of the program were achieved.

2. Program goals are *dependent* variables in evaluation research, the things we suspect are the effects of the program. The program itself is the major *independent* variable, which, we hope, causes the effect or program outcome. The program includes the people being served, the staff, the methods used, and so on. It is sometimes helpful to list the program goals and the components of the program on a chart. Goals should be listed under the title "dependent variables," and program components should be listed under the title "independent variables."

3. A number of different types of goals have been identified. There are *proximate*, short-range goals, and *ultimate*, longer-term goals. Programs usually have *multiple* goals.

4. *Program goals* should be distinguished from *practice objectives*. Especially in counseling programs, there are some goals you may have for a particular case that do not generalize to all cases in the program. In that instance, a practice objective may not be a program goal. Examining objectives in an individual case is sometimes a good way to uncover program goals.

5. The researcher needs to be sensitive to any goals achieved that were *unanticipated* at the beginning of the program or at the start of the program evaluation. The researcher should feel free to report on any information about unanticipated outcomes in the final evaluation report.

6. It is helpful to think of ultimate program goals as changes in knowledge, attitude, skill, or behavior. The researcher should think about whether the program being evaluated has these types of goals. You will almost always find goals that reflect changes in knowledge, attitude, skill, or behavior.

7. While issue of reliability and validity are given less prominence in evaluation research than in basic research, the researcher needs to be aware of these issues. The use of instruments from other research studies that have been tested for reliability is one way to solve issues of reliability and validity. By paying attention to the measurement process itself and to the questions you will ask by pretesting your instrument, you are heading in the right direction for achieving reliability. Grounding your measures in theory will give you a good start for achieving validity.

8. Program monitoring is an important part of the field of program evaluation. Monitoring implies studying program operations rather than program goals. In program monitoring, you usually ask simple questions about the program, such as, How many clients were seen? What were their problems? The results of monitoring studies are more easily fed back into the program for planning purposes.

EXERCISES FOR THIS CHAPTER

1. For a social program you are acquainted with, make a list of dependent variables or goals for the program. Then make a list of all the independent variables, the program itself, the intervention, the characteristics and so on.

2. Take a piece of paper and draw a line horizontally across the top of the paper. Write the heading "proximate goals" on the left-hand side of the line and the heading "ultimate goals" on the right-hand side of the line. Think of the goals of a program you know about and list them by deciding where they belong along the continuum.

3. Take the case situation of an individual or a family you may see in treatment or pretend you or your family receive treatment. List the treatment or practice goals for the particular family or individual. Indicate which of the goals could be generalized to a group of individuals or families who may be in a treatment program and which goals would probably be idiosyncratic to that one case.

4. Take a concept such as self-esteem, anxiety, attitude toward disability, or marital satisfaction. Indicate the kinds of questions you would ask to operationalize the concept you have chosen.

REFERENCES

Bradshaw, J. (1980). *The family fund*. London: Routledge Kegan Paul.

Frankfather, D., Smith, M.J., & Caro, F.G. (1981). *Family care of the elderly*. Lexington, MA: D.C. Heath & Co.

Jayaratne, S., & Levy, R. (1979). *Empirical clinical practice*. New York: Columbia University Press.

Kiresuk, T.J., & Sherman, R.E. (1968). Goal attainment scaling: A general method for evaluating comprehensive mental health programs. *Community Mental Health Journal*, 4(6), 443–453.

Kogan, L.S., & Shyne, A.W. (1966). "Tender-minded and tough-minded approaches in evaluation research." *Welfare In Review*, 55(2), 12–17.

Patton, M.Q. (1988). *Qualitative evaluation methods*. Beverly Hills, CA: Sage Publications, 329–332.

Rosenberg, M. (1965). *Society and the adolescent self-image*. Princeton, NJ: Princeton University Press.

Rossi, P.H., & Freeman, H.E. (1989). *Evaluation: A systematic approach*. Beverly Hills, CA: Sage Publications.

Scriven, M. (1967). The methodology of evaluation. In R. Tyler, R.M. Gagne, M. Scriven (eds.) *Perspectives of curriculum development* (pp. 39–83). Chicago: Rand McNally.

Suchman, E.A. (1967). *Evaluative research*. New York: Russell Sage Foundation.

Weiss, C.H. (1972). *Evaluation research: methods of assessing program effectiveness*. Englewood Cliffs, NJ: Prentice-Hall.

5 The Third Step: Designing the Study

DESIGNING THE STUDY

After the researcher determines which program goals to study and describes and defines the goals, he or she must complete the plan for the study. This plan or *study design* describes how you will answer the research questions about whether the program achieved its goals. The study design has four parts: (1) selecting a research design; (2) deciding how to collect data; (3) constructing a data collection instrument; and (4) selecting a sample of people to interview or the parts of the program to observe.

There are two ways in which design is used here. The *study design* is the overall design of the research study, which includes four parts of planning the study. Selecting a *research design* is the first part of the overall study design. The *research design* is the logic of how you will answer the research questions. You specify whether you will conduct a survey interviewing clients *after* the program, whether you will interview or test clients both *before* and *after* the program, or whether you will conduct an *experimental study* to compare two different forms of the program.

Having a plan or an overall study design is crucial for research. In implementing their first research study, students in the human services usually say, "I will select a few clients to interview and directly observe the program." But, a much more specific plan is needed in selecting a research design, collecting data. and so forth.

Why is developing the plan important? By developing the plan you specify the systematic method you will use to answer the research question.

These systematic procedures, based upon the methods of social science research, are what distinguishes research from other processes. Applying the
principles of design, data collection, and sampling in the program setting is
what distinguishes research from other methods of practice or administration in the human services.

A study design also is important because one decision, such as what
type of data collection you will use, sets in motion a series of steps you must
take into account in planning the study. For example, if you design a study in
which you will conduct personal interviews with 100 people who received
service, you must create the personal interview form, schedule interviews,
and hire interviewers. You know that by using a personal interview you can
ask more open-ended questions because the interviewer can probe to clarify
the response. If you decide to hand out the questionnaire, you must ask more
close-ended or yes–no types of questions. In each case, you must construct a
certain type of instrument and select a sample of people to interview. The
study design or plan describes how you will do all this.

A famous movie director once said that in order to film a movie
everything must be planned in detail before you go out to shoot the movie.
He realized that some things will go wrong once you go out to film, but you
must anticipate as many contingencies as you can in your plan *before* you
start shooting the movie. It is the same in social science research. Your study
design helps you anticipate what you must do to conduct the research study.

In the human services, if you are doing direct treatment or providing
service, you need a plan for how you will proceed. If you are doing group
work, you will need a plan for what you hope to do with your groups. If you
are teaching, you need a curriculum plan as a guide. In research, the same is
true, *you need a plan or a study design.*

SELECTING A RESEARCH DESIGN

In selecting a research design or in specifying a logic for the study, the three
simplest forms of design are presented. The first is a survey design or an *ex
post facto* study. The second is a pre-post study. The third is an experimental
study. There are many other research designs (Tripodi, 1983), but these are
the simplest and most common forms of design for program evaluation.

Survey Design

The simplest and most commonly used design in the social sciences is a
survey design. In a survey, data collection usually takes place *ex post facto* or
"after the fact" of the program. The easiest example to use is a study where

you conduct follow-up interviews or handout questionnaires to 50 clients at the conclusion of the program. You would select an *ex post facto* design when you want to examine program outcome from the perspective of a client or a human service worker.

Survey research is the type of research most generally used by market researchers. For example, they ask you questions about the kind of toothpaste you are using *after* you have selected it and *after* you have used it. Merely substitute the word program for toothpaste and you understand the idea of the survey approach in program evaluation.

A survey design has many strengths. It is a relatively simple, all-purpose design. It generates sound, systematic data in relation to the reactions of people to the program and any changes they think they may have experienced in the program. It is a strong design if you want to determine how clients, workers, or administrators have experienced the program, what they think about different parts of the program, and what they think are the effects of the program. It can frequently generate enough data so that we can examine relationships between the characteristics of the participants in the program, the type of intervention they received, and their perceptions of the program and its possible effects.

Survey designs are especially good in the beginning stages of evaluating a program when less is know about the program. It is best to use when no evaluation of the program has ever been done, and no client or worker has ever been formally interviewed about the program. It is also a good way to initiate program evaluation because you have completed the preliminary steps of describing the program, describing program methods, and defining program goals. This will produce more knowledge about the program in the setting in which you are working.

The limitations of the survey approach are in examining cause-and-effect relationships between the program and its goals. We can determine what effects people *seemed* to experience as a result of the program. However, since we did not interview people *before* the program, we have no baseline data on where they were initially. Therefore, we have no real data on change.

Pre–Post Design

This second limitation of an *ex post facto* study, the lack of baseline data, can be corrected by using a second type of design, the pre–post design. In a pre–post study, there is an interview or observation *before* the program (sometimes referred to as the pre-test) and an interview or observation *after* the program (sometimes referred to as the post–test). This is an improvement on the *ex post facto* survey because you can monitor changes in the client's situation. An example of when this type of design might be employed would be a training program where one of the goals is to increase a person's knowledge of community resources or a program where a goal might be to increase a person's knowledge of AIDS. The pre-test alone also may have great potential as a needs-assessment device. For example, if we administered a pretest on a person's knowledge of AIDS or of community resources, it would tell us what people in our program need to know in order to gain more knowledge.

The pre–post study is also essentially a survey, however, it adds change data to the *ex post facto* survey. We can compare changes in knowledge, attitude, behaviors, and skill from the time before the program to the time right after the program. In addition, this design has all the advantages of the *ex post facto* design. Usually, the interview or test before the program contains questions that will be asked again at the end of the program. The interview after the program will contain both the post-test and additional information about a person's reaction to the program. Thus, the pre–post study can also gather all the data that were useful in a survey design for reactions and experiences with the program and can reveal what the participants thought about the effects of the program. Background information and characteristics about the client can be asked in the pre-test. In a *pre–post* study, two observations provide much more information for program evaluation than the *ex post facto* study, which is also referred to as a one-shot study. The cost of data collection, however, can double and more resources are needed.

Experimental Design

The third type of research design is an experimental design. The major purpose of experimental design is to establish cause-and-effect relationships between the program and the program goals. Experimental design involves randomly allocating people to different forms of intervention or program, into two *contrast groups*. An example is a program in a child welfare agency for parents who are known to abuse their children. To test the effectiveness of two different forms of treatment, parents would be randomly allocated to two different modes of treatment. One form of treatment might be psychoanalytically oriented counseling. Another form of treatment might be a parent training group using behavior-modification techniques. As clients are referred for treatment, the first client would be given the counseling; the second would be given the parent training; the third, counseling; the fourth the parent training; and so on, until there a substantial number of clients in each group.

Many experimental studies also contain a *control group*, which is studied but is not treated. This is done so that treatment can be contrasted with no treatment to determine the program's effects.

The theory behind experimental studies is that the random allocation of clients should produce two groups of clients who are similar in all respects, except for the fact that they received two different forms of treatment. In experimental studies, we come the closest to finding *cause-and-effect* relationships. Similar to the pre–post study, initial, baseline data on the clients' characteristics and their abusive behavior would be taken *before* the program, and observations on the clients' abusive behavior would be taken *after* the program. Pre–post observations could be compared for both groups, and the *changes* that took place in each group of clients could be compared to determine if the counseling groups or the parent training groups were more effective.

The above example points out one of the major disadvantagess of experimental design. The biggest problems are the ethical issues brought about by random allocation. We randomly assign people to different forms of the program because we are more likely to achieve equivalent groups. This means that cases are allocated by chance rather than by the decision-making of professionals. Human service practitioners, however, are taught that they should make a diagnosis and determine which form of treatment might be better. This type of design creates conflict between human service workers and researchers. For example, the worker might believe that a case allocated to counseling should be given to the parent group or vice versa. Clients, too, are less powerful in experimental studies as they are not given the choice of one form of treatment over the other. There are many who say that the form of treatment given in experimental studies is not "real" treatment because it is not the usual form of service whereby the worker refers a client to a particular form of service and the client is also active in choosing a particular form of treatment.

Ethical problems are created by a control group for which treatment is withheld. Sometimes a control group can be created more humanely from clients waiting to enter the program, and concerns about using control groups can be reduced by not withholding treatment that would normally be given. Generally, the use of a contrast group, in which a different form of the program is given, is considered more ethical than the use of a pure control group where treatment is withheld.

In experimental studies, if it is hypothesized that one form of treatment will produce better results, the client is not supposed to know in which of the two groups change is expected. If the client knows that the researchers except improvement, he or she may "think" the condition is improving simply because it is supposed to improve. This is called "the Hawthorne effect." When the client does not know in which group change is expected, this is called a blind experiment. Research staff too can be subjected to this bias. Thus, for example, when research staff interview clients, they should not know which group the client is in or whether the study hypothesizes that one form of the program is better. This is called a double-blind experiment. Experimental researchers frequently conduct debriefing interviews with the subjects and/or the research staff after the study to determine how much they really know about the study and whether what they knew affected their responses or behavior.

A second example of an experimental study is a study of inpatients in a psychiatric hospital who are released to residential aftercare programs. Patients could be randomly allocated to two different aftercare residences or halfway houses. In one of the halfway houses the major treatment method might be intensive counseling. The second residence might offer milieu therapy as the major type of treatment. Psychosocial assessments and standardized testing in areas of life functioning would be made *before* their release from the hospital and again *after* their release from the hospital, after six months in the residential program. Comparisons would then be made on *changes* in the two groups to determine if the counseling or the milieu therapy had a greater effect.

In this last example, the experimental design seems to fit the evaluation of this type of program and it may be more likely to initiate an experimental design to as to examine cause-and-effect relationships. Patients are released to these two programs anyway and, by randomly allocating them, we are more likely to produce two groups that are similar except for their type of residential program.

If random allocation is considered to be unethical, we might use the model of experimental design without random assignment to assess the program. The discharge workers in the hospital would be allowed to use their normal practice to refer the patients to the appropriate program. The clients too could be active in this decision-making process.

As a class of studies, experimental studies without random allocation are called *quasi-experimental* designs. When we have a situation where the model of experimental design fits but we do not randomly allocate cases, we call this a *naturalistic experiment*.

Another example of a naturalistic experiment is when a training program has two different forms of training. For example, in an AIDS training program, we might have one group where factual information is provided and another group where some sensitizing group experience is provided in addition to the factual information. The researcher does not want to allocate people randomly to the two groups, but uses experimental design as a design model. The design is similar to the pre–post but its purpose primarily is to test differences in the outcomes of the two approaches in a cause-and-effect manner.

The real value of experimental design is that it allows you to introduce a model about which you can discuss the ultimate effectiveness of programs and can raise issues of causality. This model encourages us to think about how *ex post facto* and *pre–post* studies fall short in terms of studying ultimate effectiveness.

Experimental studies also are useful in introducing the idea of a *contrast group* to examine the relative effectiveness of different forms or levels of the program. This notion of a contrast group is useful even in an *ex post facto* survey. For example, similar to the way you looked at two different forms of aftercare in an experimental study, *ex post facto* studies can analyze two different groups of the people in the same program. For example, you could create contrast groups of those who attended less of the program—5 out of 10 sessions—and those who attended more of the program—9 out of 10 of the 10 sessions. We can then see if different levels of exposure to the program produced different levels of goal achievement. By examining the relative effectiveness of the two groups we can *infer* causal connections between the level of program and what was achieved. The overall model is that different people, given different levels of the program, will have different experiences with the program and achieve different levels of outcome.

We should not think that experimenal studies are the ultimate goal of all evaluation research or the highest form of research. While the value of *ex post facto* studies was in generating good descriptions of programs, in experimental studies, less resources are spent describing the program and more resources are spent on tests and measurements to show ultimate effectiveness. For example, in the naturalistic experiment we discussed in the evaluation of the treatment of patients leaving a psychiatric hospital, the design assumes we have some reliable and valid measures of life functioning to compare the two groups in relation to outcome.

Since experimental studies examine ultimate effectiveness, they are often preferred by governmental funding sources as a method of ultimate accountability. However, we should never overlook the knowledge-building, accountability and consumerism potential of *ex post facto* surveys or of *pre–post* studies.

DECIDING HOW TO COLLECT DATA

How do you construct a plan for data collection? First, you must decide what type of data you will use to evaluate the program. Will you use primary sources, such as a personal interview, or mail or hand-out questionnaire for a client, a family member, or someone providing the service? Will you directly observe the program or some part of the program in operation? Will you use secondary sources, such as case records, or information such as management information system reports, court reports, or school records? etc. These are possible data collection procedures and instruments that you might consider.

There are a variety of ways to collect data in research. Each particular method has its own advantages and disadvantages, which must be weighed. However, when the practical circumstances under which it is *possible* to collect research data are reviewed, usually only one or two choices emerge as the most reasonable choices.

PRIMARY METHODS OF DATA COLLECTION

There are two main methods of data collection you might utilize to evaluate the program. The first and most commonly used methods are primary methods. These include personal interviews, questionnaires that you mail or hand-out, or direct observation of the program.

Primary methods are called *primary* because you are directly observing the program or you are collecting original or primary data by interviewing or testing people who have direct contact with the program—the staff, the people who were served, the administrators of the program, and so on.

The researcher generally has more *control* over the data collection process when primary methods are utilized. He or she formulates the questions for the interview and plans the process by which the interviews are conducted. This process includes constructing the questionnaire, training and hiring the interviewers, assuring the quality of data collected, and so on. This is in contrast to the researcher who uses secondary methods of collecting data by relying on case records, court reports, or hospital records.

Personal Interviews and Questionnaires

The usual method for collecting research data is through personal interviews or questionnaries. Two decisions are involved here. First, should you use a personal interview or a questionnaire? Second, who should be interviewed?

The term "personal interview" is usually reserved for an in-person contact where you ask someone questions related to the program goals. Personal interviews are the most flexible form of data collection. Having a person ask the questions allows the interviewer to probe for a depth of response. This means you can obtain the affective content of people's response to the program. Since social programs are such complex endeavors, responses to how the service was delivered can usually best be obtained in personal interviews. Both open-ended and checklist and scale items can be asked within the same interview with good results. Of course, having the personal interaction means that you must ensure that your interviewer is not putting words into people's mouths and is asking questions in a uniform manner from interview to interview.

Personal interviews are much more expensive than handing out or mailing an interview form. It costs money to hire an interviewer, set up the interviews, conduct the interview, and write the answers to open-ended questions in a clear fashion.

Mailed or handed-out questionnaires are considered as impersonal approaches to data collection. The advantage of questionnaires is that they can be inexpensively administered. However, the response rate is usually a problem. People experienced with mailed questionnaires know that one of the best response rates may be approximately 65 %. The problem is that you do not know how the 35 % who did not respond felt about the program. If only 25 people attended the program, under the best of circumstances you may get only 16 respondents.

Questionnaires should not depend primarily on open-ended questions because people generally will not give in-depth responses if someone is not present to ask them to expand their responses. Structured, close-ended questions are generally more productive in questionnaires. In addition, questionnaires are usually more productive with literate, knowledgeable, and motivated respondents.

Sometimes, the researcher can use techniques that have the advantages of both the personal interview and the questionnaire. For example, for a group of people who have just completed a program, you might give them time to complete the questionnaire while they are at the program to increase the response rate. Also, you might point out the open-ended questions and ask people for thoughtful responses. Or, you could conduct phone interviews, which would bypass the costs of sending out an interviewer and would retain some of the personal interaction of an in-person interview.

Who To Interview

In program evaluation the type of people you can interview for the purposes of collecting data is limited. Primary among those you may interview are the clients of the program or their family members, the professionals or service workers who provide the service, and the program's administrators.

The people who receive the service sometimes know best about the effects of the program. These are the people who were taught, trained, given counseling, and referred to programs for service. They know what was done, what was worked on, when the service was offered, and if the service offered was what they needed. Many social programs, however, do not listen to clients. Yet, clients are thought to be the main beneficiaries of programs and the ones who experience the outcome or effect of service. If the purpose of the program is to increase a person's self-esteem, we might administer a self-esteem scale before and after the training to determine in what ways self-esteem has changed. Along with this, we may ask a number of questions after the program which are directly related to how the client experienced the service. In this way we are capturing both ultimate goals and the subjective interpretations of the people served.

Certainly, if you want to know who are the best teachers in a particular school, you start by asking the students—the people who experience the classes every day. This is why you usually ask your friends about a teacher before you register for a particular course. While what they say may be entwined with other things, such as who is "easier," other students are usually the best sources of who might be the best teacher. However, we would not only be interested in these subjective reactions as data for evaluating teachers, but we also would administer tests to the students in various classes to determine more ultimate measures of teaching competence.

Gaining access to the people served after they receive service usually means that confidentiality must be maintained and that clients may have the right to refuse to participate. This procedure may be a little more rigorous than if staff were interviewed. After all, it is a matter of public record that staff participate in the service but this might not be so with clients.

Client interviews and responses on tests may be especially problematic with disabled groups. Schizophrenics or seriously developmentally disabled persons would be especially difficult subjects to interview. However, we must realize how important it is to interview these groups, because they may be the only people who experienced the program directly. We should not let our prejudices or stereotypes deter us from at least attempting to interview disabled people about the program. In some cases, for example, if program participants are very young children, we may have to rely on parents or family members as respondents. Or, we may encounter programs whose intent is to change whole families or programs where the family is the client and we must choose who to interview or conduct a family interview.

An additional source of data or an alternate source are the service providers. Staff or human service professionals can provide useful feedback from their perspectives. Questions addressed to the staff require their judgment: What is their judgment about the outcome or the progress of clients during the service? In contrast to clients, human service professionals sometimes have greater knowledge about the proximate goals that can be achieved and greater knowledge about the techniques used in service and the possible effects. They may know what parts of the program did and did not work.

Professionals are especially comfortable in the interview situation and are usually quite verbal (you may even have to cut them off). They also are usually good respondents if you simply give them a questionnaire to complete. It is generally easier to gain access to workers than clients, and many of them consider it their professional responsibilities to help evaluate the service.

Direct Observation of the Program

Besides interviewing someone, the researcher may choose to directly observe the program in operation. So, for example, the researcher may choose to observe the process of the groups designed to increase socialization of the elderly in a senior center to determine which types of socialization the program seems to be improving. Or, a training program can be observed to determine how the curriculum design is working. Direct observation of one-to-one clinical practice still may be less palatable, except in some facilities where devices such as one-way mirrors have gained acceptance.

Direct observation tends by its nature to be a less structured approach to data collection. It is critical in direct observation that the researcher has some idea beforehand what he or she will observe. For example, in direct observation of the groups at a senior center, the researcher should determine what areas of socialization were the focus of the program. Next would follow a period of direct observation during which the researcher would make copious process notes based upon that observation. Then the researcher can compare the themes in his notes to the areas originally outlined to see if the program was addressing the issues that it set out to address. By analyzing these process notes (which will be discussed as qualitative data analysis in the next chapter), the researcher can also determine if the socialization behavior of the seniors will be changed or affected by the program.

Direct observation can sometimes be more structured. For example, in a program designed to have parents interact more with their children, the researcher can observe parent-child interaction in a playgroup situation and set up rules for recording the number of times the parent and child interacted.

However, data from direct observation are more often qualitative process notes about what went on in a particular program. Such data are more subjectively analyzed. Nonetheless, it can provide rich, descriptive data, especially for programs in their more formative stages of development.

SECONDARY METHODS OF DATA COLLECTION

Secondary methods of data collection are methods in which the data were *not obtained primarily* to help document the effects of the program. Examples of secondary methods are: the case records of professionals who provided the service, the academic records of those who participated in a school-based program, court records and reports that document further criminal activity or delinquency, or hospital records that indicate whether the mentally ill patient was rehospitalized.

At first glance, using secondary sources to document the effects of a program is quite appealing. The researcher does not hire anyone and can simply construct questions, consult the records, and see what happened to program participants. However, the research questions you can answer are limited by the data *available* in the records and the reliability of secondary sources is often low. Professionals often do not keep good case records. Administrative reports are often completed in a hurried fashion or inaccurately. More often, the data you expect to find from these records simply are not there. If there are serious gaps you may find that from the 50 people who attended the program, you can find records or data on only 25 of them. Relying solely on secondary data can seriously affect the ability to carry out program evaluation.

While reliance solely on secondary sources is usually difficult, there are certain instances where available data can be especially helpful. For example, if you evaluate a program in the schools, you might want to use existing data on students' standardized tests to determine if the program effected students' academic progress, or you might want to use reports on the students' behavior when they were in the program or shortly after the program. If you conduct a study under the auspices of the probation department or the courts, you may have easier access to reports and can determine the reliability of court records and probation reports. If you conduct an exploratory study on the early stages of a program, you might want to use the professional's case records as a source of data. If you are conducting research in the same setting where the records are located, you may be more successful in obtaining complete data on those records.

Because of issues in the reliability and quality of secondary sources, a good rule of thumb is to use these sources as *one* minor method for assessing the program's success. Since it is often a more inexpensive form of data collection it is often appealing to use secondary sources as the major source of data collection. If you do this, you may find that you lack data on the program's success. That can be a nightmare for the beginning researcher. More seasoned researchers are wary of secondary sources and generally use this method as a backup to primary sources such as personal interviews. For example, in a school-counseling program you may use interviews with the students as a primary data source as well as records of student academic progress and records of the students' behavior at the school.

While the researcher need not construct an interview when using secondary methods, a data collection form needs to be developed to help transfer data from the records to data on forms that can be analyzed for research purposes.

CONSTRUCTING THE DATA COLLECTION INSTRUMENT

Once the type of data collection is decided upon and you choose either to interview people or to observe the program you must construct a data collection instrument. This step follows logically from the previous stages of program evaluation where you described the program and defined the goals of the program. The data collection instrument needs to contain questions that ask for the respondents' background characteristics such as age and sex etcetera, questions that are related to their experiences with the program, and questions that *operationalize* the goals of the program.

This section will illustrate a data collection instrument used to evaluate an employee assistance program. Examples of correct and incorrect ways to frame questions will be discussed. The principles of questionnaire construction are summarized at the end of this section.

The data collection questionnaire also shows how client characteristics, various parts of a program, and the program goals, or *the dependent variables* are operationalized. In other words, you will see how a series of questions are created to measure these variables and concepts.

A CASE EXAMPLE FROM AN EMPLOYEE ASSISTANCE PROGRAM

A major university developed and operated an employee assistance program for over two years and wanted to evaluate their beginning efforts. The program was planned to serve all employees of the university and provided counseling for family and individual problems, referral to services needed by the employees, counseling for problems about job stress, alcoholism, drug addiction, help with children in the family, and help with an aged member of the family, among other services.

As one part of program accountability, the program developed a management information system to record the kinds of problems employees brought to the program and to record which types of employees—faculty, administrative staff, secretarial, or custodial staff—used the program. (See Appendix B.) As another part of program evaluation, program staff decided to conduct an evaluative study as one beginning method for determining the outcome of the program.

A *study design* was developed for the overall study. First, a *research design* was chosen. A follow-up study, an *ex post facto* design was chosen because some beginning questions about service delivery and outcome needed to be answered. Because a variety of client problems were represented it was difficult to isolate goals that could be measured across cases in a *pre–post* design.

In the second step of creating a study design, a type of data collection was selected. A personal interview would have been the best method of data collection, but program policies made it inadvisable to conduct a personal interview. One of the policies in this employee assistance program was to maintain strict confidentiality so that university administrators do not have access to case records. Therefore, if a faculty member, administrator, or secretary comes with a drinking problem this does not become part of their personnel file. This policy presented the evaluator with difficult problems in implementing an evaluative study. A personal interview would represent too much of an invasion of the confidentiality principle. Even with a mailed questionnaire, you could not risk sending a questionnaire to the employee's department, which might compromise the principle of confidentiality. Nor could the questionnaire be sent home.

A decision was made to select a group of employees who had frequent, usually once a week, contact with the program for counseling over a period of at least six months. The questionnaire was to be handed to the employee by the social worker who counseled that person. The questionnaire was to be mailed back to the program in an addressed, stamped enveloped that was provided.

The third step of the study design was to *construct the data collection instrument*, or the questionnaire. Because people completed the questionnaire by themselves, the instructions had to be extremely clear. Because the questionnaire format was chosen, the researcher was aware that most of the questions had to be in the close-ended, checklist format since it was not possible to probe for in-depth responses. (The complete client satisfaction questionnaire used in the study appears in Appendix C.)

The interview or questionnaire always needs to begin with an introduction. The introduction should contain the general purpose of why the study is being conducted, how long the interview will take, and the confidential nature of the interview, and assurance that participation in the study is purely voluntary. Here is the introduction to the employee assistance program follow-up study questionnaire:

UNIVERSITY EMPLOYEE ASSISTANCE PROGRAM
CLIENT SATISFACTION QUESTIONNAIRE

The Employee Assistance Program would like to know if we have served you well. Please take five minutes to tell us about your experience with the service by answering the following questions.

Note that this information is completely confidential. Do not put your name on this questionnaire. Notice too that we do not ask you any identifying information such as the department where you work, your position at the University, or any information such as age, marital status, etc.

When you have completed the questionnaire, simply place it in the mailbox.

Your candid responses to the following questions will help us at the program improve services to you and your fellow employees. Thank you.

Notice that the client was not told that the study was purely voluntary. The researcher may have violated the principles of the protection and treatment of human subjects. Since the client was *only* being handed the questionnaire, the researcher assumed that the client would not think that he or she was being pressured into participating in the study. Also, since questionnaires have a low return rate to begin with, the researcher thought that giving the right of refusal might have jeopardized getting any responses back. This is a good example of how a principle might have been violated or may have been compromised to implement the study. The decision of a review committee on the treatment of human subjects should have been instituted to determine whether principles were violated.

Most questionnaires ask for the characteristics of the respondents. The characteristics are important because we usually are interested in the relative success or failure of the program with different groups of clients. The history of program development and program evaluation indicates that, in fact, program success varies for different groups of clients. Note that in this questionnaire no demographics were asked for so that the respondent would realize that *strict* confidentiality was being maintained. To illustrate the kinds of client characteristics that could have been studied, items from the facesheet that workers complete when someone comes to the program are presented here:

Gender of Client: male ____   female ____

Ethnic characteristics: ____ White, non-Hispanic

                        ____ White, Hispanic

                        ____ Black, non-Hispanic

                        ____ Asian

                        ____ Other (list) _____

Age: ____ years

Position in the University: ____ Faculty ____ Administrative

                            ____ Secretarial ____ Custodial,
                                                  Maintenance

 Notice that the above are examples of categories, which are used in close-ended questions. There are two principles to be followed for the categories in close-ended questions. First, the categories must be mutually exclusive. They cannot overlap. For example, the categories of administrative and secretarial jobs do overlap. In that situation, it might be better to ask job title and job responsibilities and have research staff make these finer distinctions of who is in a secretarial position and who is in an administrative job.

 The second principle is that categories must also be exhaustive. Close-ended categories must include all the possibilities. The categories for position in the university should also include a category for "other" where people can write their position if it does not fit the given categories. A laboratory assistant working in the university would have no category to check off if a special category or an "other" category were not included. This would make the categories exhaustive. Since laboratory assistants made up only a very small part of the university population, "other" could be used rather than creating a special category of laboratory assistant.

 After the introduction, basic questions were asked about the program experience. These questions represent the operationalization of the independent variables, such as the problems of the employees, how they discovered the program, the number of times they met with the social worker, the type of intervention given, and how the employees' problems may have affected their job performance. These questions should be introduced to the client in a *natural flow* of events as they occurred during the program. These should begin with "What brought you to the program?" and proceed with questions such as, "What did the program do for you?" and "Did it help you?"

The following close-ended items were included in the questionnaire to measure the program variables. They are examples of how to use structured checklists correctly, especially in reporting problems that brought a person to service.

Employee Problems

1. Which of the following best describe the kind of situation or problem for which you sought help at the Employee Assistance Program? (Check as many as apply.)

____ Trouble getting along with a spouse or someone with whom you share a close personal relationship.

____ Trouble with a child in your family.

____ Trouble getting along with a family member or friend.

____ Stress from a change in living circumstances.

____ Trouble carrying out responsibilities at home.

____ Physical or health problems.

____ Financial problems.

____ Trouble carrying out responsibilities at home.

____ Trouble getting along with someone at work (e.g., co-worker or supervisor).

____ General irritability at work.

____ Trouble dealing with feelings or emotions.

____ Drinking or drug problems.

____ Other; please describe _____

Notice that a structured, close-ended problem checklist was used because this is a questionnaire. If people were asked to describe their problems, they may have chosen not to respond or would not have given comprehensive descriptions. Notice too that the instructions are clear and that the wording of questions is in simple, everyday language, free of professional jargon. The alternative would be to include items framed in jargon. Suppose you saw the following checklist items:

_____ neurotic tendencies

_____ acting-out child

_____ symbiotic relationship with my mother

The respondent might not know the meaning of these terms. More important, perceptions of neurotic tendencies makes the question and the answer somewhat ambiguous. One person's notion of "neurotic tendencies" might be another person's ideas of normal behavior.

Notice too that the results of such a checklist can be analyzed in a number of ways. First, did a particular client have a problem or not, such as general irritability, at work? Second, you can look at clients' combinations of problems. Third, you may look at the total number of the clients' problems as another piece of quantitative data.

To develop a natural, time-ordered flow, initial questions asked about the client's early program experience. Question 3 shows how we can ask about the concept of *referral* in clear and simple words. We might ask, "Who *referred* you to the program?" However, a better way to ask it would be the following:

3. Did anyone suggest that you go to the Employee Assistance Program?

_____ No

_____ Yes, a co-worker

_____ Yes, my supervisor

_____ Yes, someone else, e.g. family member, personal friend, etc., please list their relationship to you (not their actual name)

_____

Questions 6 and 7 also asked about the service clients were given in the program.

6. What would you say the EAP staff person did for you?

7. How frequently did you meet with the EAP staff person?

_____ once a month

_____ about every other week

_____ about once a month

_____ less frequently than once a month

Surprise, in Question 6 an open-ended question was used. Notice that open-ended questions can be used in a handed-out questionnaire. However, a good rule of thumb is not to have more than 30% of your questions be open-ended. Also, the questions asked in open format should not be key questions for which you need responses from everyone. In the above question, some general idea of what the professional did was needed and the major focus of the study was not on worker techniques. Notice too that asking *some* open-ended questions in a handed-out questionnaire makes for a more realistic and natural interview that flows from one question to the next in a non-mechanical way.

Although a pre–post study was not selected, some questions may be asked about the client's situation *before* the program, even if you are asking after the fact. In a pre–post study, we might have a number of tests and measures of dependent variables, such as job satisfaction and ability to concentrate, which we measure before and after the program. In an *ex post facto* study, we may create a proxy premeasure of what the person thought about their level on the dependent variable before the program.

Question 2 illustrates the use of questions to establish the client's status before the program even if it is collected in the post-questionnaire.

2. Was the problem that brought you to the Employee Assistance Program negatively affecting your experience at work in the following ways? (Please make a check for every question.)

A.	less satisfaction from my job	____ Yes	____ No	____ Somewhat
B.	reduced ability to concentrate at work	____ Yes	____ No	____ Somewhat
C.	more absences or lateness	____ Yes	____ No	____ Somewhat
D.	not doing my work as well as I usually do	____ Yes	____ No	____ Somewhat
E.	trouble getting along with others at work	____ Yes	____ No	____ Somewhat

A series of questions were designed as operational indicators of the dependent variables that represented the goals of the program. Questions 4, 5, 8, 9, 10 and 12 reflected indicators of proximate program goals. These questions asked about the employee's opinion of the service that was offered, the responsiveness and convenience of the service, satisfaction with the frequency of contact, and overall satisfaction with the service.

4. In your opinion, did the Employee Assistance Program respond to your particular problem quickly?

_____ Yes

_____ No

_____ Somewhat

If no or somewhat, please explain: _____

_____

5. Was the EAP staff person available at a time convenient for you?

_____ Yes

_____ No

If no, please explain: _____

_____

8. Were you satisfied with how often the EAP staff person met with you?

_____ Yes

_____ No, would have liked less frequent contacts

_____ No, would have liked more frequent contacts

9. How helpful would you say the EAP staff were to you?

_____ extremely helpful

_____ somewhat helpful

_____ not particularly helpful

10. Specifically, what did the EAP staff person do for you that was helpful or not helpful?

Notice that Question 9 is a global judgment about the helpfulness of staff. The reliability of such a global judgment is usually a problem. In other words, someone might have checked that the staff were helpful. Following with a question that asks specifically what the staff did was helpful or not helpful can enhance the reliability of information on the first global judgment. To answer, the client might point to the supportiveness of the staff or to the particular practice techniques. This would be useful descriptive information to have and increases our confidence in the results of the global judgment question.

12. In general, what do you think of the service that you received from the Employee Assistance Program?

____ very satisfied

____ satisfied

____ neither satisfied nor dissatisfied

____ dissatisfied

____ very dissatisfied

Question 12 is a good example of a "balanced" scale item. If the item was unbalanced it might look like this:

12. In general, what do you think about the service you received from the Employee Assistance Program?

____ very satisfied

____ somewhat satisfied

Obviously, this question does not allow for a negative response.

More ultimate goals for the service were operationalized as increases in job performance, better self-concept, and improvements in the employee's personal and home life. One could envision a more comprehensive evaluation that used *reliable* and *valid* scales on job performance, self-concept, and personal life. These measures could be used before and after the program to establish possible changes in these areas. In this study, these goals were operationalized through a series of single checklist items, questions 11, 13, 14 and 15, which were designed to reflect possible changes in these areas of the employee's life.

Question 11 uses a *comparative framework* in which the client judges possible changes in the problem. A *comparative scale item* is especially useful to use in an *ex post facto* study. With the lack of measures before the program, people can be asked "if they thought" there was change as an initial indicator of possible changes.

11. How did you feel your situation or problem has changed since you first contacted the EAP?

____ become much better

____ become a little better

____ not much change

____ become a little worse

____ become much worse

Why do you say this? _____

_____

13. Did the Employee Assistance Program make you feel better about yourself in any way?

_____ Yes _____ No _____ Somewhat

A better self-concept or self-image could be operationalized in other ways through a number of *Likert* scale items, which measure the intensity of a person's attitude or feeling about himself or herself. These rating statements include:

	Strongly agree	Agree	Disagree	Strongly disagree
I feel good about myself	_____	_____	_____	_____

A Likert scale on self-concept might include 25 items that are scored—4 for strongly agree and 1 for strongly disagree—and added for a total scale score ranging from 100 (25×4) for someone who strongly agreed with every item and had a high self-concept to 25 (25×1) for someone who strongly disagreed with every item and had a low self-concept.

14. Did the Employee Assistance Program make a difference in your personal life?

_____ Yes _____ No _____ Somewhat

15. Did the Employee Assistance Program make a difference in your work on the job?

_____ Yes _____ No _____ Somewhat

Would you please give examples of how the program may have affected how you feel about yourself, your personal life, or your work?

Similar to the way a questionnaire needs an introduction, it also needs an ending that adds to and completes the natural flow of the interview. The questionnaire ended by asking if the employee would go back to the program with a problem or recommend the program to a friend. The questionnaire finished by asking for more general comments about the program and a thank you and final instructions about returning the questionnaire.

16. If you encountered a problem in the future, would you consider returning to the Employee Assistance Program?

_____ Yes _____ No _____ Not Sure

17. If a friend asked, would you recommend the Employee Assistance Program?

__ Yes __ No __ Not Sure

In the space below, please make any additional comments about the service that was provided to you by the Employee Assistance Program or make suggestions about new ways we might help you or others.

Thank you. We appreciate your help. Now simply place the questionnaire in the stamped envelope and mail it back to us.

Note that in the above example, although the overall thrust was close-ended questions, some questions were open-ended so that respondents could add information. However, notice that the instrument did not rely on the open-ended questions for the *major* part of the questionnaire.

SUMMARY OF THE PRINCIPLES OF
QUESTIONNAIRE CONSTRUCTION

1. Every questionnaire or interview should have a proper introductory statement. The introduction needs to explain the general reason for the study, how long the interview will take, and the confidential nature of a person's responses.

2. The introduction is usually the point at which principles on the ethical treatment of human subjects are implemented. The respondent should give his or her consent to be interviewed and should be told that participation in the study is voluntary.

3. Both questionnaires and interviews should establish a *natural flow* of human communication. In program evaluation, questions should begin with how the respondent discovered the program and focus on their initial contacts with the program and their later experiences in the program and possible effects from the program. As different content areas are introduced, the interview or questionnaire should not skip from area to area. Sensitive questions and questions about personal characteristics should be introduced later in the interview.

4. In a mailed or handed-out questionnaire, instructions must be extremely clear to avoid confusion. At least 70 % of the questions in a questionnaire must be structured, close-ended questions.

5. In a personal interview more open-ended questions can be asked. Open-ended questions should be followed-up with neutral probes (e.g., "Could you tell me more about that?" to encourage depth of response.

6. In both personal interviews and impersonal questionnaires, close-ended questions must have categories that are mutually exclusive and do not overlap. The categories must also be exhaustive and contain every logical alternative response. Close-ended questions should be balanced, for example, a rating scale item must contain the possibility for both positive and negative ratings.

7. Questions need to be presented in clear and simple language that is free of professional jargon. If the program is a counseling program, you should not ask a client about *countertransference*. You should not ask the parents of a disabled child if they have trouble getting *access* to *services*. You may find them saying, "No, I am not having trouble with *access*," but later in the interview they tell you that they have no transportation to medical services.

8. To keep the interview lively and natural, close-ended questions should be alternated and integrated with open-ended questions. The interview should resemble normal human interaction as closely as possible.

9. Comparative judgment items about changes that may have taken place between the beginning and the end of the program especially occur in *ex post facto* studies where no baseline change data is collected.

10. All questionnnaires or interviews should be *pretested* before they are used to ensure that all these principles are addressed, that the questions are clear, and so on. Notice that here pretest is used differently than the pretest used as an initial method in a pre-test study.

11. The ending of the interview is also important. Respondents should be given the opportunity to add any information that they think was overlooked. They should be thanked for their participation and told how study results will be used.

SELECTING A SAMPLE OF PEOPLE TO INTERVIEW OR PARTS OF THE PROGRAM TO OBSERVE

In addition to deciding on the data collection plan, you need a sampling plan. Sampling is utilized in research to answer the question of how to select people to be interviewed or parts of the program to be observed. Are the clients you have selected for study *representative* of all the clients in the program? This is important because you do not want to select only the most successful or the least successful cases for study. You do not want a *biased* sample. If you select 100 cases to study in a program that served 1,000 cases, you hope that those 100 cases are similar to the 1,000 cases, so that what you find in the 100 cases will be true in the remaining 900 cases.

There are two ways sampling helps us in program evaluation. First, we try to show that we have an *unbiased sample*, that we did not purposely select and the most successful or the least successful cases. A good administrator hopefully knows one or two cases that were success stories where the clients found the program very helpful. Most likely the service staff also knows these cases and they are talked about *because* they were successful. Discussing these cases with funding sources can be very helpful. However, these few case examples can only take you so far. In research, we take this extra step by trying to select an *unbiased* sample to determine whether the program was successful with the average case, client, or family. There are certain procedures we can use to help select an unbiased sample.

Second, we want to *generalize* beyond our findings. If 60% of those in our sample liked the program and our sample was representative of a larger population of all people in the program, then we would be safer in assuming that 60% of all the people liked the program. A sampling plan helps you achieve *representativeness* or *generalizability*.

Sampling in social science research is based upon two concepts—a population and a sample. A population is a larger, more inclusive group of people or cases. It may be the total number of people or human service workers in your program. For example, if you are studying the attitudes of high school teachers or social workers in New York City, the population might be *all* high school teachers or *all* social workers in New York City.

A sample is a smaller, less inclusive group of cases or individuals you will select for your study. The sample is the group of those who will be interviewed or observed. So, if you are studying the attitudes of high school teachers you will select some teachers out of the population of teachers and send them your questionnaire. Naturally, you try to get an unbiased representation of teachers. You do not only want those teachers whom you know personally in the sample. Also, you hope the group in your study is similar to the population of all teachers. Then there is a greater probability or likelihood that the attitudes of those you studied would be similar to the attitudes of the total population of teachers. Likewise, if you were studying the reactions of the students in your school to the curriculum offered, you would try to assure that you had a sample that reflected the experience of the average student in the program so that curriculum development would not be developed based on the feedback of a few atypical students.

In program evaluation, there are great benefits if we can show that it is likely that our sample is unbiased and representative of our population. When we report our findings, we can speak more assuredly. In reports to funding sources, boards of directors, client groups, or professional groups, we can say that we have the responses of the typical people served in the program. Everyone likes to be able to make some generalizations about the program as a result of our evaluation. Politicians and executives sometimes act as though they have conducted an evaluation and have achieved this level of generalizability *without having a representative sample, sometimes without even having conducted a study!* When we conduct research, we have a scientific basis for making such generalizations when we have a representative sample.

Notice that we are not talking about sure things here. The only real way to find out how all the people felt about the program would be to interview them. Sampling is based upon *probability* or a *greater likelihood* that what is true of your sample is also true of your population.

In program evaluation, sampling is a little different from that in basic research. In most cases, the population is defined as the total group of people in the program. The sample is defined as the cases or people in the program that you will select to be interviewed, observed, or otherwise included in your study. In program evaluation, the sampling plan differs somewhat if you have a small or a large program.

SMALL PROGRAMS

If you evaluate a small program, for example, 25, 50 or 100 senior citizens attending socialization groups in a senior center, you may be able to interview or handout questionnaires to everyone in the program. In this case, you can try to interview everyone, and your sample is the total population of seniors in your program. Congratulations! You have avoided the need for more complex sampling procedures. The sample of people in your study is the same as the total population.

If, for example, your groups of seniors have been in existence for over two years, you might say that the population is all 50 seniors who began in the program with the group starting on a certain date and are available for interviews. To help achieve some *generalizability* in this instance, you would want to know how the current groups compare to the previous socialization groups. For example, you would want to know how the attendance rates for the current groups compare to the attendance rates of the previous groups, what different approaches were taken in the previous groups, and any other differences that can be determined. Also, you would want to know how the characteristics of the seniors in previous groups differed from the characteristics of those in the current groups. All this information will help you put your evaluative study in a broader perspective. If you have some indication that previous and current group programs are similar there is some basis for saying that the experience of the current group may be similar to the experiences of the seniors that have entered the groups in the past. This gives you some basis for *generalizing* beyond the experience of those in the group you are evaluating.

For small programs in which your sampling plan indicates that you will interview the total population (everyone in your program), two key factors can affect your sampling plan. These two factors are *nonresponse* and *program attrition*. In fact, in small programs, nonresponse and program attrition can undermine your entire study plan. You may have so few interviews that your evaluation is reduced to the responses of a few people.

Nonresponse could greatly affect program evaluation because if only 25 out of 50 people agree to be interviewed, you will not be getting responses from 50% of your sample population. What about the 25 you could not interview? Are these the ones who are more negative or more positive about the program experience? The main point is that you will not know. Furthermore, you will only have the experiences of 25 people to analyze and it is often difficult to establish trends when conducting your data analysis.

Program attrition or people dropping out of the program, could also affect your study greatly. In theory, one should report on the experiences of all 50 seniors who *began* in the groups. If some dropped out of the group, these people also should be interviewed. Interviews with these people might also give an indication of why they dropped out of the group. If they cannot be interviewed, minimally, you can report on the characteristics of these people to try and determine how they might have differed from those who continued to the program. Needless to say, if 50 people start out in the group program and only 20 are interviewed in the last group session, the sampling plan has become seriously flawed by *program attrition*. Descriptions of program attrition are very important in program evaluation, and very crucial indicators of the success or failure of the program in themselves. Reports on program attrition are especially central for program planning issues of how many people dropped out of the program and why they may have dropped out.

PARTS OF THE PROGRAM TO OBSERVE

When you have an observational study, you may not be concerned with how a sample of clients reflects a population. You want to make sure that you observe *representative* and *unbiased* parts of the program. Observational studies most likely fit the case of small programs. If you have a group program with only 10 sessions, you may need to observe all 10 sessions. Because you have observed the total population of sessions there is no need to observe a sample of sessions that represents the population of sessions.

If you have a larger session with many more than 10 sessions, you can apply the probability and nonprobability sampling techniques we will discuss shortly with large programs. The only difference is the session rather than the client becomes the unit of observation. We may select sessions randomly from the total number of sessions (a probability sample), or we may select particular sessions because they are important to the success or failure of the program (a nonprobability sample).

LARGE PROGRAMS

In large programs or programs in which you cannot interview everyone, you need sampling procedures and methods. For purposes of explanation, we will discuss drawing samples of *people* or *clients* who attended the program. For example, let us say that your socialization groups of senior citizens are serving 1,000 seniors all over the city and you want to select 250 of those seniors to be interviewed about their experiences with the program.

Here is a situation where sampling procedures can be quite helpful. In this situation, you hope to get an *unbiased* sample and one in which your sample of 250 cases will be representative of the population of 1,000 people in the program.

PROBABILITY SAMPLING

We use probability sampling techniques, first, to select people systematically, rather than in a haphazard or biased fashion. By using probability sampling techniques, there is greater possibility that we are not purposely selecting those who had an atypical (a better or worse) program experience. Probability sampling techniques are known to produce more systematic, unbiased samples. Second, it is more likely that you can assume that your sample reflects your population if you use probability sampling techniques. If we have a probability sample, we can more reasonably expect that the characteristics of the 250 seniors we have chosen are similiar to the characteristics of the 1,000 seniors in the total program (i.e., in relation to age, sex, social class, or how they experienced the program).

The simplest method for selecting a probability sample, and the one that is most appealing, is called *systematic selection*. As an example, we might take a listing of all 1,000 people in the program and select every fourth case until we had our sample of 250. This is an acceptable probability sampling procedure.

The only problem that would arise is if there is any cyclical pattern in our case listing. For example, what if every fourth case attended group A or was given service by worker B? Then, this group or worker would be disproportionately reflected in your program evaluation. Usually, however, there is not a cyclical pattern and the people in one group A would be listed after the people in group B, so that each had a similar chance to be included in our sample. Systematic selection is appealing because there are fewer steps than the alternative method, simple random sampling.

Simple random sample is the most commonly used probability sampling technique and is the basis for all the more complex sampling plans used by survey researchers, by the U.S. Bureau of the Census, the Harris Poll, and the Gallup Poll, among others. To take a simple random sample of 250 cases from 1,000, you would do the following: First, find the names or code numbers of your 1,000 cases and list and number them from 0 to 999 (we go from 0 to 999 because it is easier to work with a three digit number). Second, find a "Table of Random Numbers or Integers" in the back of a statistics textbook. The "Table of Random Numbers or Integers" is a grouping of numbers that have no order to them. You might get such a list of numbers by simply rolling dice which could go from 0 to 9. Today, computers are programmed to generate numbers randomly.

Below is a list of random numbers taken from a Table of Random Numbers:

75627
98872
18876
17453
53060

You would start at some point in the Table of Random Numbers and select people to interview. If you started in the last three columns at the top right-hand side, case #627 would be the first one to be interviewed, followed by #872, 876, 453, 060, and so on until all 250 cases are selected. What if you come up with duplicate numbers? Go on to the next number. You would not interview the same person twice.

Since the random numbers come from Table of Random Numbers the cases are selected in a systematic, unbiased manner rather than through any accidental process or any system of personal selection. The past experiences of researchers using these techniques, have taught us that they are superior in obtaining unbiased samples that are representative of your population. Others who critique our study will realize that we are less likely to have bias in our sample because we have used probability sampling techniques.

In comparing the first method, systematic selection with simple random sampling, you might have noted that systematic selection was slightly easier because you did not have to organize a population list or consult the Table of Random Numbers. For example, if you have all cases in file drawers, it is easier to pull out every tenth case and put it in your sample.

Both types of probability samples, systematic selection and simple random samples, may have three factors that create bias and can affect the degree to which the sample reflects the population in your study.

The first kind of bias comes if you do not have and *all-inclusive population list*. Simply stated, someone from your population list does not have a possibility of being included in your sample if the case is not included on your population list. As you can well imagine, record keeping in organizations often is sporadic and disorganized. Cases are left scattered about on desks or in desk drawers. Sometimes there is no list of everyone in the program so the researcher must create such a list. Creating such a list and describing the characteristics of those on the list can be a real payoff of using the systematic research method. The organization where the research is taking place will benefit. Quality program monitoring can result if we find out more about the characteristics of those in the program, how many times they came to the program, and so on.

The need for an *all-inclusive population list* is especially important for you to remember if an outside organization is auditing the services of your organization. The city controller's office may take a random sample of your organization's cases for study. However, often the population list is not all-inclusive and omits particular types of cases that have *no* possibility of being included in the study. For example, in one recent audit of home care service in New York City, the Controller's Office selected only cases from the Bronx where there was no in-service training for the home care workers. Home care professionals pointed out that the study did not reflect all home care cases in New York City, even though a random sample was selected. The Controller's report would have been more acceptable if it had recognized the limits of the sample. However, to draw headlines, the report acted as though what was true in the Bronx was true in all the five boroughs of New York City.

Program attrition is a second kind of bias that can affect probability samples. If 20% of the people dropped out of the program shortly after its beginning, you need to report that they are not part of your population list. Those who have dropped out of the program should either be part of your population list or a special group of people to be interviewed. Minimally, you need to tell people that such a group exists and we should interview them to see why they did not continue in the program. Attrition is a very important part of descriptive program information.

Nonresponse is a third factor which can cause bias in your sample. When a person who was selected in your probability sample cannot be located, or does not agree to be interviewed or does not return a questionnaire, another person must be chosen. This biases your probability sample and can cause significant error if it happens frequently. For example, if you can interview only 150 of 250 people chosen for your sample, your sampling plan has been seriously affected and it is more likely you will have a biased sample which does not reflect your population. We know this from previous attempts to draw probability samples from populations where there were high rates of nonresponse.

Can we always assume that because we have used probability sampling techniques that our sample reflects our population? No. You cannot. A good researcher finds out what the characteristics of the population are and compares the characteristics of the population to the characteristics of the sample that is selected. For example, you may find that you have fewer females in your sample than in your population or that the ages of those in your sample are younger than those in your population. Likewise, you may find that those in your sample attended the program less than those in you population. In this way, the researcher always checks on the representatives of his or her sample. Even if you find that the sample is not representative, having this information can help you speculate about whether or not these differences may have affected your evaluation findings. Reporting on the characteristics of the population in your program in itself is a very beneficial part of program evaluation for program administrators, practitioners, funding sources, and so on.

One important principle in the ethics of social research, the principle that people should voluntarily participate in the study, can affect a probability sample. If people refuse to participate in the study, this increases nonresponse and means that the original person selected for the study must be replaced by another person. Also, the choice of data collection procedure affects nonresponse which, in turn affects your ability to get a representative sample. Nonresponse would naturally be larger in mailed or handed-out questionnaires than it might be in personal interviews. Nonresponse would be greater for mailed questionnaires than for questionnaires handed-out during a program in a group setting where respondents are given the time to respond.

NONPROBABILITY SAMPLING

The alternative to probability sampling is *nonprobability* sampling. With nonprobability samples, we have less assurances that our sample will reflect the population, and usually the sample will not reflect the population. A good example of this is the first type of nonprobability sample, an *accidental sample*. "Accidental" sampling is as ominous as it sounds. Needless to say, a researcher does not go about bragging at a national conference that he or she has an accidental sample. In an accidental sample, you just go out and select cases or start interviewing people from the program. Generally, you may get those people who are known by staff because they are more prominent in the program or are having more successful program experiences. If you are interviewing those in a senior center or a community center, you may get those who are "hanging out" and making use or different use of the program than the usual person. The important point is that you have no way of knowing who these people represent because you have not organized a population list or selected a sample in a systematic way.

Usually with an accidental sample, the sample will not reflect your population. Also, in studies using nonprobability samples, you are less likely to see reports of the characteristics of your population because a population list has not been organized as the procedure is less systematic. For example, you are less likely in studies with nonprobability samples to see reports about the personal characteristics of those in the program or about their attendance or other facts about their participation or lack of participation.

Another type of nonprobability sample is a *quota sample*. In a quota sample, you make sure you have enough of the kinds of cases you want to do your analysis. For example in a school-based counseling program for 100 adolescents you may want to interview 25 male and 25 female adolescents to see if the program had a different impact for males than females. Although we have introduced more system to our sample in selecting on the basis of gender, you still have a nonprobability sample that was selected in a somewhat haphazard fashion. The good news is that your sample will help you determine if males had a different program outcome than females. The bad news is that your sample is most likely not representative of a larger population of those in the program.

Another type of nonprobability sample is a *purposive sample* in which we try to select people who would be representative of the population of those in the program (on the basis of sex, age, race, program experience, and so on). While it might seem like this would be easy to do, experience with samples in social research has taught us that this is hard to do. Using your own good judgment is not as systematic and orderly or as scientific as selecting a probability sample.

Is there any value in nonprobability samples? The answer is a strong yes. Even though you may have a biased sample and there are stronger possibililities that your sample will not reflect the total population of people in the program, at least you are evaluating the program by selecting *some* people or cases who were in the program. Interviewing one person about the program with a standard set of questions is better than not interviewing anyone, regardless of whether or not they are representative of all those in the program. Interviewing 5 people is better than interviewing one person and interviewing 25 people is better than interviewing 5 people even if you have a nonprobability sample.

More often we see programs with no evaluation. So it is better to start some orientation to evaluation than to worry or be immobilized because you only have a nonprobability sample. Even if you are selecting the people who are more positive about the program, at least you have found some success cases. If you do not know who they represent in terms of a larger population of cases, or even if you have a biased sample, at least you are evaluating the program for the first time. You are following up to see if people valued the program or workers thought the program had strong points or flaws, and you are achieving some of the goals set in the first chapter, namely, accountability, knowledge-building, and consumerism.

SAMPLE SIZE

This brings us to the question of how many people we need in a sample. Certainly it is better to have enough people to establish some trends in the data. So given limited resources, do as many interviews as you can. In a small program of 25 or 50 people you should try to interview everyone. The best way to understand the limits of a small sample is to think about whether or not it would be misleading to use a percent figure in analyzing data. If we have only 5 cases in the total sample each case would represent 20%. It would be misleading to say that 60% liked the program because we are talking about only 3 cases. If we have 25 cases, each case represents 4% so that if 60% liked the program, we are at least talking about 15 cases. Likewise with 50 cases, 60% is 30 cases. So a minimum number to be interviewed might be 25, 50, and so on.

In larger programs, there are some guidelines for determining how large a sample you need. What should be the maximum number in the sample? There are two principles that can guide us here (Backstrom & Hursh, 1963). The first principle that applies: *the more people we can interview the better.* Second, sampling theory tells us that there is a *point of diminishing returns,* a point beyond which there is no value in interviewing more people. It should be noted that this point only exists for programs with a large population.

Here is an illustration of both principles on the basis sampling theory. A program serves 1,000 people. If we interview 100 people, we might have a sampling error rate of plus or minus 10%. This could mean that if 60% of those in our sample liked the program, the percent of those in the population who liked the program could range from 50% to 70%. This error rate is usually considered a little high, and our sample would not reflect our population.

If you select a sample of 280, your error rate might be reduced to only plus or minus 5%. In other words, by interviewing 180 more people, we cut our error rate in half. If 60% of those 280 interviewed like the program, the population figure for all 1,000 people in the program might be 55% or 65% who liked the program. Not bad, you say. So what if you wanted to reduce the error rate by another 3% to plus minus 2%. Well, you would have to increase the size of your sample from 280 to 715, an increase of 435 more people who you must interview. You need to interview over 435 more people to reduce the error rate by 3%. In this example, 280 was the point of diminishing returns, and increasing the sample beyond 280 was not likely worth the extra effort and expense.

The following chart, based upon the mathematical formula for computing error rates, will give you estimates of how large a sample you would need with a population of 1,000:

Population of 1,000 Clients	Error Rate	Results in Sample	Results in population
interview 100 clients through random sampling	+ or − 10%	60% of 100 interviewed liked program	50 or 70% liked program
interview 280 clients through random sampling	+ or −5%	60% of 280 interviewed liked program	55 or 65% liked program
interview 715 clients through random sampling	+ or − 3%	60% of 715 interviewed liked program	57 or 63% liked program

The study depicted on the above chart would be affected by other types of error such as measurement error about the reliability of a measure of a person's attitude about the program.

Also, sampling theory is much more complex than the above example suggests. The example cited above is true in principle, however, when it comes to actually doing a study with a large population, comparisons should always be made between the sample and the population to see how much of a discrepancy there may be between the sample and the population in relation to certain characteristics. For example, we would want to know the sociodemographic characteristics of the 1,000 cases so we can determine how similar or dissimilar they may be to the sociodemographic characteristics of the 280 cases. Such data are an important indirect benefit of conducting program evaluation.

SUMMARY OF KEY IDEAS IN THIS CHAPTER

1. The researcher must develop a plan or an overall study design to conduct program evaluation properly. In the plan, the researcher specifies how the standardized procedures of social science research will be implemented.
2. Designing the study includes four parts:
   (1) Selecting a research design.
   (2) Deciding how to collect data.
   (3) Constructing a data collection instrument.
   (4) Selecting a sample of people to interview or parts of the program to observe.
3. The three major types of research design for program evaluation are *ex post facto* surveys, pre–post studies, and experimental designs.
4. The survey design is a simple, all-purpose design. It is useful for documenting in a systematic manner client and worker experiences in the program.

5. The pre–post study is the most useful design for studying *change* in programs where the goal is to produce change in particular areas.

6. Experimental design, when it fits the situation, is the best way to examine cause and effect relationships between the program and its outcome. Random assignment, which is a key feature of experimental design, can create serious ethical problems.

7. No one design type is the best. The researcher should select the design that fits the situation. It is also possible to mix types of designs. For example, you can carry out a survey in the post-test of a pre-post study; or, you can use the model of experimental design to help *infer* the cause and effect relationships between different levels of program intervention and different outcomes.

8. The major methods of collecting data are primary methods such as personal interviews, questionnaires or direct observation of the program. The researcher must also determine *who* would be the most likely source of data about the program—the client, the client's family, the human service worker, the administrator, and so on. If direct observation is chosen, the researcher needs to be clear about *what* will be observed.

9. Secondary methods of data collection include case records, school reports, and court reports, among others. If secondary methods are used, the researcher must make sure that the data are recorded in a complete and systematic manner. Case records and agency reports are often incomplete and inaccurate.

10. The researcher takes the final step in operationalizing the program and the program goals when the data collection instrument is created. In constructing data collection instruments, the principles for good data collection should be consulted (see pages 92–93).

11. The researcher needs to make sure that he or she selects an unbiased sample of people to be interviewed. The sample selected for the study should also reflect the population of all the people in the program.

12. Sampling in program evaluation differs if you are evaluating a small or a large program. In a small program, your sample might be your total population, and you should try to interview everyone. In large programs, probability samples are usually better to use than nonprobability samples.

EXERCISES FOR THIS CHAPTER

1. Describe three programs—one in which a survey design would be the most appropriate form of evaluation; one in which a pre-post design would be most appropriate; and, one in which an experiment or a natural experiment would be more appropriate.

2. Describe a situation in which primary methods of evaluation could be used. Describe a situation in which you would have faith in secondary methods.

3. Make up questions for a questionnaire that use complex, professional language. Show how such questions might be asked more appropriately using clear and simple language.

4. Go through the steps involved in selecting a random sample of 200 clients from a population of 600 cases. What kinds of problems does a random sample help you overcome?

REFERENCES

Backstrom, C.H., & Hursh, G.D. (1963). *Survey research*. Evanston IL: North-western University Press. See, especially, 32–34.

Tripodi, T. (1983). *Evaluative Research for Social Workers*. Englewood Cliffs, N.J.: Prentice-Hall. See, especially, "Research Designs for Evaluating Social Programs," 145–159.

6

The Fourth and Fifth Steps: Implementing the Program Evaluation and Analyzing the Data

IMPLEMENTING THE PROGRAM EVALUATION

At this point it is good to look back on how far you have gone in program evaluation. You started by realizing that program evaluation is a critical professional activity. You have described the program. You defined and operationalized program goals. You have planned the study by: selecting a study design, planning a data collection strategy, constructing a data collection instrument and selecting a sample of people to be interviewed. While all this seems very detailed, the plan of the study *must* be well thought out because once you go out and start implementing the study anything can happen and usually does.

In the fourth step, you go out and collect the data. You collect the data according to your plan by either administering the questionnaires or interviews or directly observing the program, or collecting data from case records or the institution's records about the program. Implementing the study plan and collecting data might involve training interviewers, if personal or phone interviews are to be done, or duplicating questionnaires and mailing them or handing them out. You try to insure that your response is adequate for the study you are conducting. You check to make sure your interviewers are asking questions clearly and recording the answers in a legible manner. In handed-out questionnaires, you make sure that people are listening to the directions in the questionnaire and answering all the questions properly. You start examining the quality of the data as your interviews are completed or returned.

Just one example of the problems in implementation is illustrated by a researcher who was conducting a study of the relationships between the aged and their families. The researcher tried to obtain a sample by asking for volunteers in a senior citizens center. The researcher set up coffee and danish for those who would participate in a meeting where they would fill out the questionnaire. Participation was voluntary. Unfortunately, very few people chose to participate in the study. Not only was it difficult to obtain a sample, the researcher wound up eating the danish and gained ten pounds.

These are the kinds of problems that can arise when you go out into the field. Clearly, some changes had to be made in the study plan to insure a sample of study participants. This is merely one example of the kinds of obstacles that can occur as one goes out into the field.

Often, the data collection process becomes modified in some way when the study plan is implemented. One hundred personal interviews may be needed but funds may have run out and only 75 interviews could be conducted. Interviewers may not be hired in time and the study thus delayed. Many people may refuse to participate in the study and only 50 of a total population of 100 in the program could be interviewed. These deviations from the plan are similar to what happens in practice where a practice plan is developed but could not be implemented. For example, where family counseling is the recommended course of treatment but only one person from the family is willing to participate in the therapy. While research requires even more adherence to the plan than practice, some changes always occur in the implementation phase and these changes should be mentioned in the final report.

Through persistence and personal commitment you usually overcome obstacles in the field to complete the data collection process. Now, do not be like the doctoral student who told his adviser his dissertation was completed and came in and plopped 200 completed questionnaires on the adviser's desk. Obviously, you suspect that you need to do something more than this. However, at this point you are saying to yourself: "What the heck do I do with this stuff now?"

Now comes one of the two last steps in program evaluation. In the sixth step, you must *analyze* the data you have collected. The balance of this chapter will explain how to do this in a very simplified and concrete manner.

DEFINITION OF DATA ANALYSIS

It takes time and creative skill to present data in a readable form that adheres to the principles of good data analysis. The purpose of data analysis in program evaluation is to compile and summarize the data you have collected so that you can determine whether or not the goals of the program have been achieved. Most often we are looking to find some *formative* conclusions about the program. Formative conclusions are more short range conclusions that help determine what efforts should be made to improve the functioning and efficiency of the program (Scriven, 1967). For instance, out of analyzing data from program evaluation, you may discover that the program is most effective with cases from a certain referral source, and these are cases where more success is achieved.

Less often, we are concerned with *summative* conclusions, that is, does the program work, is it effective in total? Should it be refunded? Often a service is being provided for a social problem that needs to be resolved, and the question is often how to change a program in a formative manner to help a particular group of people rather than starting over from scratch.

TYPES OF DATA ANALYSIS

For purposes of explanation, data analysis will be divided into two types, quantitative data analysis and qualitative data analysis. The concept of the two different types of data analysis is really quite simple. Quantitative data analysis techniques will help you determine what to do with close-ended questions, checklist types of data, scales, number of years, and number of service contacts. In other words, any data that is structured can be put into numerical form.

You will need the techniques of qualitative data analysis when analyzing open-ended questions, process notes from training programs or group programs, descriptive paragraph-form records, case examples and other types of non-quantitative data.

In both quantitative and qualitative analysis, the *importance of having a plan for data analysis cannot be overlooked.* The most important evaluative questions should be analyzed first. Which of the program goals were achieved and which were not? What factors helped the program achieve its goals?

Quantitative Data Analysis

Once you have collected data in which you asked people structured questions, you need to know how to analyze it. The first step in quantitative data analysis is the examination of frequency distributions. A frequency distribution is a fancy term for an aggregation of the responses of the people you interviewed. In other words, how many answered yes or no? How many agreed or disagreed? How many thought the program was very helpful, somewhat helpful, or not helpful?

TABLE 6.1 Employee's Perception of Whether Program Helped

	Number	Percent
Helpful	19	47%
Not helpful	21	53%
	40	100%

As an example, what if you had conducted the followup study described in the previous chapter for the university employee assistance program. You received questionnaires from 40 employees who had used the program. One of the questions in the interview was: "Was the program helpful in assisting you with your problem?" No fancy data analysis facilities are available for this study. So, the first thing you do is put the 40 interviews in a pile and take one blank interview and tally all of the responses on the blank interview.

After tabulating the data, a simple frequency distribution for this question could be presented in a table such as Table 6.1. This should take the mystery out of what a frequency distribution is. It is simply an adding up of the results of the answers to a specific question. Notice that the number of responses add up to 40. Also, you will usually see a percentage figure included in a frequency distribution table. If someone told you merely that 19 employees found the program helpful, you would say, "What does that mean? Nineteen out of how many?" A percentage is a simple statistic that shows what a number means in relation to the total group that responded. Knowing that almost half of the employees, 47% of the total group, found the program helpful gives us a clearer perspective on the results than knowing that 19 employees found the program helpful.

In addition to percentages for categorical, close-ended questions, a mode can be used as a measure of central tendency. The mode is the typical response or the most frequently mentioned response category. If 30 out of the 40 people thought the program was not helpful, then "not helpful" would be the modal category. In the data where 19 people thought the program was helpful and 21 did not, technically "not helpful" was the modal category. However, to use the mode where no one category had clearly the largest number of responses would be somewhat misleading.

Usually a table similiar to Table 6.1 would be presented in the findings and the table would be referred to in the text which described the findings. The text accompanying the findings might look like this:

About half of these employees thought that they had been helped and about half thought the program did not help them. Nineteen of the 40 employees (47%) said that the program was helpful to them (Table 6.1). Twenty-one (53%) said that the program was not helpful to them.

If you had 35 closed-ended questions such as this one, you could theoretically have 35 such tables when you report your findings. Of course it would be repetitious to have 35 frequency tables in your report. Not every structured question needs a table. The text reporting the data might be enough. Tables are useful when the categories are complex and can be read more easily if they are in a table. Also, having the data two places, in the table and the text, can be helpful because it reinforces a finding, especially if it is a key finding.

The power of presenting these simple frequency distributions is often overlooked by the beginning researcher. Yet it is a most important first step. The average person's image of research is that it looks for relationships among variables. The beginning researcher frequently rushes to examine relationships between variables and questions before presenting the simple, most basic data. I call the tendency to pursue interrelationships among variables before the initial data is presented "premature cross-tabulation."

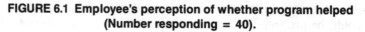

FIGURE 6.1 Employee's perception of whether program helped (Number responding = 40).

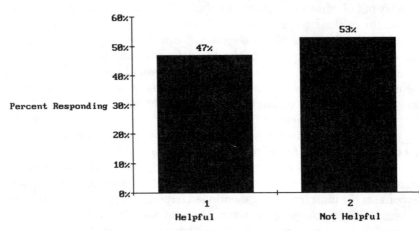

The power of presenting simple frequency distributions can be greatly enhanced through the use of graphics. The data from Table 6.1 are presented in a bar chart in Figure 6.1 and a circle or pie chart in Figure 6.2. The researcher should choose the particular graphic representation that displays the data most accurately and convincingly. For this data, with two discrete categories, the bar chart seems to work the best. Note that this bar graph uses the number responding as the axis on the left side. In the bar chart, the percents should be included at the end of each bar display. Pie charts are better when you have more categories and you are especially interested in showing the data from the base of 100%. Notice that percentage figures were used in both graphs in addition to the visual display. The accessibility of graphic programs on the microcomputer nowadays will greatly increase their use in program evaluation reports (Tufte, 1983).

FIGURE 6.2 Employee's perception of whether program helped (Number responding = 40).

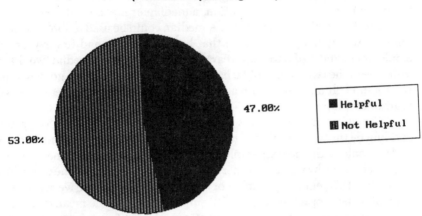

In addition to the quantitative analysis of categorical data from the results of your study and the use of simple percents, variables that are not categorical can be presented with simple measures of central tendency—usually the median and/or the mean. Suppose for the 40 employees who responded you had data on how many years they were employed:

Number of years at the university	Number
1	9
2	5
3	3
4	1
5	6
6	3
7	4
8	2
9	3
10	4
	40

In the above data, there are so many categories for years at the university that the number of people at a particular year does not tell you much. For data that is continuous such as age, years, income, number of contacts, etc., summary statistics such as the median or mean are needed.

A mode that is the most frequent category could be used to show that the most frequently reported number of years at the university was 1 year of employment. Nine employees were employed for one year. However, the mode is more appropriate with categorical data (under 5 years, five to ten years, etc.). In the above distribution, a median or mean would be a better measure of central tendency to use. A median could be used to show the person that was typical in the sense that half the people had fewer years of employment and half had more years. In this example, the median would be in-between the two groups of 20 cases. Adding up cases as you go down the right-hand column until you reach 20 you will note that the median was 5 years of employment.

The mean or average was computed by adding up all the years and dividing by the total number of people in the study. Notice that the first row had 9 people with one year employment or a total of 9 years. The next row had 5 people with two years' experience or 10 years in all. The next row had 3 people with 3 years employment or 9 years in all. In all there were 191 years of employment represented by the 40 employees so that the mean or average was 191 years divided by 40 people or an average of 4.8 years employment at the university. Measures of central tendency are important for any continuous or what is called an interval level variable, such as, number of years, number of children, number of contacts, and age. (Those measures where you have a measurable and distinct difference between one, two, or three, e.g., years of age, hours of service.)

Cross-tabulation

After the frequency distributions on single variables are examined and univariate analysis is conducted, then relationships among variables should be examined. The most common mode of analyzing the relationships between two categorical variables or close-ended questions is cross-tabulation.

In the example we used above, we would be especially interested in determining who were the employees that thought the program helped and who thought it did not help. One obvious factor we might look at is the type of problem they brought to the program. Let's say one group came with problems relating to their self-esteem and a second group came with marital problems. We would then look at the relationship between those two variables—whether they thought the program was helpful and the type of problem they had. Each respondent would then be cross-classified by "helpful"

TABLE 6.2 Helpfulness of Program by Employee's Problem

	Marital problem		Self-esteem problem		Total
	n	%	n	%	
Helpful	4	20%	15	75%	19
Not helpful	16	80%	5	25%	21
	20	100%	20	100%	40

or "not helpful" and "self-esteem" or "marital problem." In other words, you would examine the 19 who thought the program was helpful and find out which of these employees had come for service with self-esteem problems and which had marital problems. Then you would look at the group of 21 who did not think the program was helpful and find out which of them had self-esteem problems and which had marital problems. If the data were analyzed by computer, you could simply ask for the cross-tabulation of these two variables in the data set and the computer would cross-classify on the responses of these two questions for respondent 1, respondent 2, and so on, to respondent 40.

The results would be presented in a table such as Table 6.2. It turned out that 20 of the 40 had marital problems and 20 had problems with self-esteem. Notice that each respondent was classified into one of the four categories or cells on this table. Notice too that the type of problem, the independent variable, was chosen as the column variable (up and down). Whether they found the program helpful, the dependent or outcome variable, was selected as the row variable (across). Percentages were computed based upon the independent variable, that is, the 20 with self-esteem problems and the 20 with marital problems was used as the base of 100%.

As you have noticed, cross-tabulation tables are much more difficult to read and interpret than univariate or simple frequency distribution tables. The text interpreting the cross-tabulation table might look like the following:

> Those employees with marital problems found the program much less helpful than those with self-esteem problems. While only 20% of those with marital problems found the program helpful, 75% of the employees with self-esteem problems said the program was helpful. Likewise, 80% of those with marital problems reported that the program was not helpful and only 25% of those with self-esteem problems found the program was not helpful.

Graphic representation of cross-tabulation data in a stacked bar chart aids greatly in understanding the data. In Figure 6.3, you see that different shadings were used for those who found the program helpful or not helpful within each column of those with marital or self-esteem problems.

FIGURE 6.3 Helpfulness of program by employee's problem.

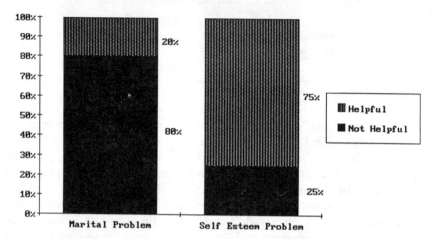

While a cross-tabulation is more difficult to interpret than simple frequencies, this one did show a fairly clear trend. More often such tables do not show trends as clear as this one. Even in this table we know descriptively there is a trend, but how do we know if the researcher's interpretation of a trend is correct or not? Is it purely the researcher's values that are operating? Is he or she making it look as though there is a relationship between the two variables when there is no trend? This is a very important decision-making point in research. For one thing, each person reading the study has the data to examine and the data sometimes shows a clear descriptive trend.

There are also other indicators that we use to determine whether there is a relationship between two variables or not. This is why we use tests of statistical significance.

Tests of Statistical Significance

Tests of statistical significance enable us to tell if there is a relationship between two or more variables based upon more than the researcher's own interpretation of whether or not a relationship exists. When we use a significance test, we are using probability theory to determine if there is a relationship or not. We are not just making a subjective judgment about whether or not there is a relationship between two variables.

Technically, tests of statistical significance are used to *infer* whether or not a relationship that exists in the study sample would exist in the population from which the sample came. In program evaluation, this would be the situation if I had a random, probability sample of 200 seniors from a population of 1,000 who attended socialization groups for the elderly. We might want to examine increased socialization as a goal of the program. One of the relationships among variables we might examine is the relationship between the age of the seniors and increased socialization. We might expect that the program would be more successful at increasing the socialization of the young elderly rather than the older elderly. If we found a statistically significant relation between age and increased socialization among the 100 seniors in the study we would be able to infer that such a relationship exists in the population of 1,000 elderly.

Technically, this is what it means to have a statistically significant relationship between two variables. However, if you remember our discussion of sampling from the last chapter, you know that often in program evaluation we do not have a probability sample from a population. Although mathematical statisticians warn us that using significance tests without a probability sample from a population is incorrect, social scientists seem to use these tests as a standard against which to assess whether a relationship between two variables exists or not. Tests of statistical significance are used to help us determine whether we have a *chance* relationship or a real relationship between two variables.

The most common statistical test of significance which would most likely be used for the data in Table 6.2 is a chi-square test. If a chi-square test was used, you would see the following figures at the bottom of the table when it is presented:

$$x^2 = 12.12, df = 1, p < .001$$

The $p < .001$ at the end is the most important part of the statistical test for purposes of interpretation. This is the p-level or probability level which tells you whether or not the test is statistically significant. $p < .001$ means the relationship was statistically significant. Technically, it means that there is less than one chance out of 1,000 that the association between the two variables could have been found arrived at purely by chance. In other words, there *was* an association between these two variables.

Any p-level below .05 means that technically you have a statistically significant relationship between the two variables. Note that smaller is better in this instance. P less than .05 means there is less than a 5 percent chance that the relationship between the two variables could have been arrived at purely by chance. Chance is based on probability or what you would normally expect. In other words, when the probability of a relationship between two variables is less than chance, less than a 5 percent chance, there *is* a statistically significant relationship between the two variables.

A common p level that is also reported is $p < .01$, this, too is less than .05 and statistically significant. P less than .01 means that there is only one chance out of 100 that the relationship could have been arrived at purely by chance. In other words, there is a statistically significant relationship.

The probability level is one part of a statistical test of significance. It is the most important part because it interprets whether or not the relationship is statistically significant. In most statistical tests, you will see the p-level which is used to judge the end result of whether the variables are related or not. So the p-level is one common factor you can look at when you examine statistical tests in studies.

The first part of the statistical test is the test statistic and there are different test statistics used under different situations. The most commonly used test statistic for an association between two categorical variables is chi-square. This is the $\chi^2 = 12.12$ which was reported earlier.

Unlike the p level where smaller is "better." For test statistics, larger is "better". The larger the chi-square, the more likely the association is statistically significant, i.e., the smaller the p-level we will find.

Chi-square involves a comparison between the frequencies we have in our cross-tabulation table called the *observed frequencies* and the frequencies we would get if there were no association between the two variables, called the *expected frequencies*.

Computation of chi-square

To show the meaning of chi-square one will be computed here. Note that such computations no longer have to be completed by hand as they are done by computer nowadays.

Chi-square is a test of association between two categorical variables. The statistical definition of chi-square looks like this:

$$\chi^2 = \sum \frac{(o-e)^2}{e} \text{ for each cell.}$$

This formula says that chi-square equals Σ (sigma) or the sum of the observed (o) minus the expected (e) frequencies. Note that the observed minus expected frequencies are summed or added *for each cell* in the table. In the EAP example, there were four such cells. The *observed* frequencies were those frequencies I observed when I did my study. These frequencies are listed below in the four cells of the table. They are 4, 15, 16, 5:

Observed Frequencies

	Marital	Self-Esteem	Total
Helpful	4	15	19
Not Helpful	16	5	21
	20	20	40

So, in the above table, 4, 15, 16, and 5 are the observed frequencies or what I found when I did the cross-tabulation.

To compute a chi-square five steps are necessary:

Step 1—Examine the observed frequencies in my table, 4, 15, 16, and 5.

Step 2—Compute the *expected* frequencies for each cell in my table. The expected frequencies are what I would have *expected* if there was no relationship between the two variables. In chi-square, I am comparing how much the *observed* frequencies differ from would have been *expected* if there was no relationship between the two variables. If what I observed or found in my study differs from what would be expected if there was no relationship between the two variables, the chi-square will be larger and there would be a greater chance of a statistically significant association between the two variables.

The expected frequencies for each cell in my table are computed by multiplying the column total by the row total and dividing by the total number. Columns are up and down. You remember Greek columns, such as Doric, Ionic. Rows are across as all you gardeners know. The formula for an expected frequency is:

$$e \text{ (expected frequency)} = \frac{r \text{ (row total)} \times c \text{ (column total)}}{\text{total number}}$$

Looking at the table, the expected frequency for my first cell would be $\frac{19 \times 20}{40} = 9.5$.

The expected frequency for the second cell is $\frac{19 \times 20}{40} = 9.5$.

Note that the expected frequencies just happen to be similar because you had similar numbers for the column totals, 20 in each group with marital or self-esteem problems. This is not usually the case. You usually get different expected frequencies in each cell:

The expected for the third cell in the table is $\frac{21 \times 20}{40} = 10.5$.

The expected frequency for the fourth cell in the table is $\frac{21 \times 20}{40} = 10.5$.

Step 3—Make a table showing both the expected and observed frequences:

Table of Observed and Expected Frequencies

	Marital Problem		Self-Esteem Problem		
	Observed	Expected	Observed	Expected	Total
Helpful	4	9.5	15	9.5	19
Not Helpful	16	10.5	5	10.5	21
	20	20	20	20	40

The larger the difference between what I *observed* in my study and what I would have *expected* if there was no association between the two variables, the larger my chi-square value will be *and* the more likely there will be an association between the two variables.

Step 4—Based on the information in the above table, I can now compute my chi-square using the formula:

$$\chi^2 = \sum \frac{(o-e)^2}{e} \text{ for each cell.}$$

For the first cell, the formula would be:

$$\frac{(4 - 9.5)^2}{9.5} = \frac{(-5.5)^2}{9.5} = 3.18$$

For the second cell, the formula would be:

$$\frac{(15 - 9.5)^2}{9.5} = \frac{(-5.5)^2}{9.5} = 3.18$$

For the third cell, the formula would be:

$$\frac{(16 - 10.5)^2}{10.5} = \frac{(-5.5)^2}{10.5} = 2.88$$

For the fourth cell, the formula would be:

$$\frac{(5 - 10.5)^2}{10.5} = \frac{(-5.5)^2}{10.5} = 2.88$$

I complete the formula by adding the values 3.18 + 3.18 + 2.88 + 2.88 = 12.12, which is my chi-square value.

Step 5—Now that I have the chi-square value, I need to find the *p*-level. Nowadays the computer gives the *p*-level along with the computation. What we do is compare our chi-square value with the probability distribution of chi-square to determine what the *p*-level is. The probability distribution of chi-square is given below:

Probability Distribution of Chi-square

Degrees of freedom	Probability Levels				
	.10	.05	.02	.01	.001
1	2.70	3.84	5.41	6.64	10.83
2	4.60	5.99	7.82	9.21	13.82
3	6.25	7.81	9.83	11.34	16.27
4	7.78	9.49	11.67	13.28	18.46

The values in the table 2.70, 3.84, 5.41, reading across are chi-square values. You need a chi-square value larger than that in the table for the chi-square to be significant at the p-levels listed at the top of the columns. Note the degrees of freedom, the column at the far left, 1,2,3,4. You need to find the degrees of freedom before finding the p-level. The degrees of freedom is one way we take the number of cells into account.

If there are more cells in a table, there are more possibilities for difference so we must take that into account. The degrees of freedom are defined as the number of rows in the table minus one times the number of columns in the table minus one. In our table there were 2 rows, so 2 minus one equals one. There were also two columns so two minus one equals one. One times one is one so there was 1 degree of freedom.

Now you are ready to find the p-level. Notice that for the table with one degree of freedom, reading the first row across that our chi-square value of 12.12 was larger than the chi-square value of 10.83, so that p was less than .001. So we can say our p-level is less than .001. Remember this is what we reported earlier when we put chi-square = 12.12, $df = 1$, $p < .001$ at the end of our table.

At this point, you might be saying what is so magical about $p < .05$ or $p < .01$. There is nothing magical. It is based on probability theory. Many social scientists have raised question about the use of .05 as the standard probability level for statistical significance.

Other social scientists have argued that practical significance may be more important than statistical significance. In other words, the fact that you have some relationship even if it is not a statistically significant relationship may have implications for the program and may have real significance in terms of planning for the future. (Morrison & Henkel, 1970).

T-Tests and Analysis of Variance

As we said before, there are different statistical tests of significance for different situations. In situation where you have two categorical variables you would most commonly use chi-square. What if you had one continuous variable such as years of age, number of times people attended the program, people's score on a self-esteem scale or a marital relations scale, etc. and one categorical variable such as male-female, program helpful-not helpful, etc. In that instance we would use a *t*-test rather than chi-square.

We will use an example from the child welfare training program discussed in the third chapter. In that study, child welfare workers who had experience conducting review conferences were given a number of Likert scale items to assess their attitudes about review conferences. These conferences were theoretically supposed to help workers focus more on biological parents who are often the forgotten people in the child welfare system. The conferences were supposed to get all the parties involved in planning for the child's return home to the biological parent.

In the training program for review conferences, attitudes toward the conference were considered to be extremely important. Worker attitudes were measured on a number of Likert scale items. For example, the workers were asked to give their opinions about the following statement:

	Strongly disagree	Disagree	Slightly disagree	Slightly agree	Agree	Strongly agree
	1	2	3	4	5	6
Service Review Conferences are the best thing to happen to the child welfare field in a long time.	_____	_____	_____	_____	_____	_____

This Likert scale item was examined as a continuous variable on a scale from 1 to 6. A score of six would mean that the worker "strongly agreed" that service review conferences are the best thing to happen to the child welfare field in a long time. A score of one would mean that a worker "strongly disagreed" that conferences were the best thing to happen to the child welfare field in a long time.

It should be noted that Likert Scales are more properly applied to a group of items added together than one individual scale item and that the reliability of such scales needs to be addressed.

As one part of the study, we were interested in finding out which workers were more positive about the conferences. One aspect of this was whether the worker played a leadership role at conferences or not. Table 6.3 shows the data analysis that used a *t*-test to see if there was a statistically significant relationship between the two variables.

TABLE 6.3 Attitude toward Conferences by Whether Worker Led Conference or Not

	Mean Score	*t*-value	*p*-level*
Lead Conference (*n*=15)	4.0	2.34	< .05
Did Not Lead			
Conference (*n*=9)	2.7		

*for two-tailed test.

Again we can look at the *p*-level and see if there was a statistically significant relationship between the two variables. Looking at the *p*-level column at the end of Table 3, you see that *p* was less than .05. Thus there *was* a statistically significant relationship between attitudes toward the conference and whether or not they lead a conference.

The *t*-test was based upon differences in the mean scores of the two groups, those who lead the conferences and those who did not. By comparing the means for the two groups, it was found that the mean score for those who led the conferences was 4.0 (which is the slightly agree category) and the score for those who did not lead conferences was 2.7 (between disagree and slightly disagree).

Notice that *t*-tests are a little easier to interpret than chi-square scores and crosstab tables. The text accompanying the table would read like this:

There was a tendency for those who lead the conferences to feel better about them. On a Likert scale item from 1 to 6 (1 for strongly disagree and 6 for strongly agree), the workers who lead the conferences were more likely to rate them positively with a mean score of 4.0. Those who did not lead the conferences rated the conferences lower with a mean score of 2.7.

Notice that the bottom of the table indicates that a two-tailed test was used. This means that the researcher did not predict which group would have a higher mean score. If the researcher predicted that the workers who lead conferences would have a higher mean score, then a one-tailed test would be used.

In the above example we have two categories with one continous variable, attitudes toward conferences. What if we have three categories or groups, those who always lead conferences, those who sometimes lead conferences, and those who never lead conferences. In that situation, you use analysis of variance and the *t*-test is not used, an *F*-test of statistical significance is computed. The findings might look something like those in Table 6.4.

TABLE 6.4 Attitude toward Conference by Leadership at Conferences

	Mean Score	F-value	p-level
Lead Conference ($n=7$)	3.5	3.46	< .05
Sometimes Lead ($n=9$)	4.3		
Do Not Lead ($n=8$) Conference	2.6		

Note that the p-level was less than .05 and the F test showed a statistically significant relationship. The following paragraph would be used to describe the findings.

> Those who always lead the conferences and those who sometimes lead them rated the conferences more positively than those who never lead conferences. Those who sometimes lead the conferences had a mean score of 4.3. Those who always lead conferences had a slightly lower mean score of 3.5 on their attitude toward the conferences. Workers who never lead a conference had the lowest mean score of 2.5 and tended to disagree that conferences were the best thing to happen to the child welfare field.

The above are examples of some of the most frequently used tests of statistical significance in quantitative analysis in program evaluation (For further on these tests, see Craft, 1985; Weinbach & Grinell, 1987).

QUALITATIVE DATA ANALYSIS

How do you analyze your open-ended questions, descriptive paragraphs from case records, your process notes if you are using direct observation as a major form of data analysis, or other types of noncategorical or nonnumerical data? Qualitative data analysis is a somewhat less technical exercise. There are no statistics to guide you in your analysis. There is more possibility that the researchers' values become involved in the analysis. Does this mean that qualitative analysis is not as valid or important? No.

Qualitative data can be especially useful in providing rich, descriptive data about program activites. It can provide more intimate knowledge about the details of the program and its success or lack of success. It is especially useful in guarding against the "black box" phenomenon in which researchers treat the program as an unknown. Qualitative data analysis is what you might do if you kept process notes or a diary of your professional activities and then you wanted to examine or *analyze* your professional interventions.

Let us examine two situations. If you are conducting a survey with mostly close-ended questions, how do you analyze the open-ended questions you have asked? For example, in the evaluation of the employee assistance program, the close-ended question of whether the employee assistance program was helpful or not was followed with an open-ended question of why the program was helpful or not helpful. To conduct an analysis of this question, you would look through your 40 questionnaires and write down the employees' responses on one sheet of paper where the question was written across the top. The exact quote of the person should be written completely with their identification number, respondent 1, 2, 3, etc. on this one sheet of paper.

To analyze their responses, you would look for trends and then try to proceed to group the quotes which show different trends together. For instance, you would naturally group responses of those who found the program helpful separately from those who thought the program was not helpful.

In reporting these findings, the trends you found would be reported and some of the actual key quotes of people would be listed in the report. Often, it is these key quotes which present the flavor and the depth of what people thought. An example of how to do this will be present shortly.

The second situation in qualitative analysis is where you are conducting research where qualitative analysis is your major mode of analysis. Observational research is defined here as research where you observe in the naturalistic setting rather then by conducting structured interviews. In this type of research you had defined certain kinds of trends or program experiences you wished to examine *before* you collected your data. These variables came from the goals and program processes you wished to study. Now you will determine if these trends actually were found in your data.

There are four simple steps to qualitative analysis using process notes or descriptive records (Williamson, Dalphin, & Gray, 1982, pp. 203 and 204). First, read your descriptive data, your logs, your process notes. Second, generate as many descriptive categories as possible, starting with the categories you described as important in your research plan. Third, refine your categories based upon your data. Fourth, examine the examples you have of each category. Most important, you can organize your key descriptive passages and direct quotes under each trend that it represents. Fifth, you actually report on the major trends in the data by using key quotes and descriptive passages.

The schemes and trends you generate can represent practice theory or practice examples, overall program successes or failures, practical service needs, and implications for policy and practice. It is most important that you back up your assertions of trends with quotes and data that support such trends. Having this supportive data is akin to statistical tests of significance in quantitative analysis.

An Example of Qualitative Data Analysis

An example of the use of qualitative data analysis will be presented for a small program evaluation (Smith, Caro, & McKaig, 1987). Qualitative data are especially useful to have when you are analyzing a small program. The program we will examine served only 17 families. The descriptive and qualitative findings on such a program are often more useful than percentages and statistics analyzing relationships between program interventions and goals. In fact, many statistics are not valid to use on very small samples. Descriptions of the intervention and its effects are more useful in such exploratory investigations. The purpose in such studies is to uncover the ways in which the intervention might have been useful and feed back such results in the continued planning and implementation of such programs on larger groups of people.

The program that was evaluated was a home care service which was provided under public auspice to 17 low-income families with developmentally disabled children. A needs-assessment study on 35 of these families had uncovered the tremendous impact of caring for a child with mental retardation, autism, and cerebral palsy.

The day-to-day care needs of the developmentally disabled children were uncovered through descriptions such as the one provided by the parent of a 13-year-old severely retarded child:

He cannot do anything for himself. I feed him, bathe him, dress him. I do just about everything for him. He must be fed . . . . He just can't do it. He would not drink from a cup or a glass. He uses a bottle. He does not and cannot dress himself at all. I have to bathe him. He is not toilet trained. He uses Pampers. He's in a wheelchair. It's hard for him to get in and out of the apartment because there are no elevators and I have to carry him up and down three flights of stairs. The wheelchair also has to be carried. He must be taken everywhere. It's like the umbilical cord has not been cut.

Supervision of the disabled child was a major responsibility for these parents and it was apparent that they needed a break from the intense supervision of the disabled child. One parent of a retarded child with behavior problems talked about the supervision she provided:

He needs constant supervision. He is always climbing or jumping around. He throws anything he can get his hands on through the window. He also tries to run away. As you open the door he is roving down the stairs so you have to be careful. Also, he likes to play in the oven so you have to watch him constantly. He puts toys in the refrigerator and he has clogged up the toilet several times with towels, toothbrushes, toys, etc. I don't dare fall asleep because he wakes up easily and may wander and hurt himself while I am sleeping.

To relieve the excessive burden of these parents and to provide a respite service so they could get time off from their demanding roles and get out of the house by themselves, home care service was provided to 17 families caring for disabled children.

To evaluate the impact of this service, an *ex post facto* survey of the 17 families was conducted after the home care person had been providing service. Because of the small budget available to conduct personal interviews, telephone interviews were used as the method of data collection. Telephone interviews do permit some personal interaction which meant that open-ended questions could be asked and the interviewer could probe for an in-depth response. An interview with 21 questions was developed that took about one hour to conduct. The interviewer who conducted the telephone interviews was the same person who had conducted a personal interview in the parent's home creating some rapport between the interviewer and interviewee.

Parents were asked wide-ranging questions about the positives and the negatives of the service. It was hypothesized that benefits for both the child and the parent would occur. Five questions were asked specifically about what exactly the home care professional did and what the benefits of the service might have been.

6. What does the home care person do for your child? (PROBE: Anything else?)

7. What does the home care person do for you (the parent)? (PROBE: Anything else?)

11. What do you like most about what the homemaker does?

12. What are the benefits for you? (PROBE: Anything else?)

13. What are the benefits for you child? (PROBE: Anything else?)

Notice that in four of the five questions the interviewer was instructed to use neutral probes to obtain all of the possible things that the homemaker did and all of the possible benefits of the service.

After the study was implemented and all 17 interviews were conducted, a qualitative analysis of the open-ended questions was conducted. The researcher created a pile of the 17 interviews and instructed a secretary to transcribe the responses to a particular question on one sheet of paper. So, for example, there was one sheet of paper with a heading "Question 6: What does the home care person do for your child?" Separate responses labeled respondent 1, respondent 2, respondent 3, and so on were transcribed onto this sheet of paper.

The researcher then took this one sheet of paper with responses from all 17 respondents and started to look for trends in the data or key quotes that really showed a significant aspect of the service.

The researcher then summarized the trends in the responses. In analyzing the responses to what the home care person did for the child, overall trends were reported. The home attendants helped in most all the areas of everyday care, dressing, feeding and bathing. Home attendants also helped with the supervision of the child so the parent could take a rest or get out of the home. They also took the disabled children out to the park and in a few instances escorted the child to the health clinic.

It was also possible to conduct a *content analysis* of each person's response to determine which activities the homemaker performed and which they did not in a particular case. For example, you could look at response 1 for question 6 and see if bathing was mentioned or not, and so forth.

However, the real value of qualitative research is the rich, descriptive data that it produces. Specific quotes that showed concretely what the home care person did were used in the analysis and put directly into the final report of the evaluation. For example:

The home attendant assists him with bathing and going to the bathroom. She has to cut his food, clean up after him and supervise him. She also has to watch him closely because he comes out with something new like redecorating his room or moving the TV. She also irons his clothes and plays with him. They are both playing cards right now.

She cooks his food and feeds him. If he is not dressed in the mornings when she comes here, she'll dress him. She takes him to therapy everyday. I usually go with them on Tuesday because they have a program for mothers.

He supervises them, especially when it comes to grooming. He coordinates their clothes nicely. He cooks for them sometimes and he plays with them.

She fixes his food, takes him out to the park, makes sure that he is okay until either my son or I get home. She also takes him to his doctor's appointments.

> The home attendant bathes her. . . . The worst thing I have to do is bathe her and I am so glad I don't have to do it.

One of the fascinating things about qualitative data analysis is watching the trends emerge before your eyes and being intimately involved in the data analysis and then creatively reporting on those trends. While serendipitous outcomes can be found in both quantitative and qualitative findings, more unexpected findings are uncovered in qualitative analysis. Also, qualitative analysis obviously has more subjective aspects to it, but this is known to be part of the method and the results of qualitative analysis are more frequently challenged.

> In the analysis of this data one of the unexpected findings in relation to the benefits of the service were the positive relationships that occurred between the disabled children and the home care workers. The following are examples of the illustrative quotes used in the final report to indicate the nature of such benefits:
>
>> He bathes Angel, he dresses him, he talks to him. Sometimes I can stay in my room and hear them laughing together. He meets the school bus and keeps him upstairs in the afternoon. . . . He entertains him. He tells him stories.
>>
>> She gets along well with Maria. She talks to Maria a lot and she listens. They got along fine from the start. Maria gets all the attention that she wanted and so she is happy. In fact, all the kids call the homemaker Grandma.

From the analysis of qualitative data from these 17 cases, many benefits of the home care for the child and the parent were found, also, the parents reported about getting a break from the routine and being less socially isolated. The final report of this project recommended a continuation of the project in this agency and an expansion of this service. The evaluation also uncovered many problems in the service in the quality of some of the home care that was provided and recommended ways in which these problems might be overcome in future expansion of the program. This shows the special value of qualitative methods in feeding back evaluation results to the program for future program development.

SUMMARY OF KEY IDEAS IN THIS CHAPTER

1. The fifth step in program evaluation is implementing the study. You go out and collect data. You begin administering personal interviews, training interviewers, sending the interviewers out to collect data, and so forth. You check the quality of the data to ensure that the responses are answered properly and legibly so that the data can be analyzed.

2. Inevitably, changes in the study plan occur as the study is implemented. Often this means you might not get as large a response rate as you planned or your timetable for implementing the study is delayed for some practical reason. These changes should all be noted in the final report of your study. Hopefully, these changes will not completely compromise the study plan.

3. The sixth step in program evaluation is what you do after the data are collected. You analyze the data. The purpose of data analysis is to compile and summarize data to determine how the program is operating and whether the program is fulfilling its goals and objectives.

4. Essentially, there are two types of data analysis. Quantitative data analysis will help you summarize the data in close-ended questions, rating scales and the items in rating scales, the sociodemographic characteristics of those who used the program, and so on. Qualitative data analysis will help you summarize open-ended questions in your personal interview, process notes you have made about the program, the descriptive case records of professionals, and so on.

5. The first step in quantitative data analysis is to summarize and present simple frequency distributions. How many said yes or no? How many said that the program helped them? How many agreed or disagreed with a particular attitude item? The power of presenting simple frequency distributions is often overlooked by the beginning researcher.

6. The findings from frequency distributions are usually reported descriptively in the text. Key findings can be presented in tables as well as being described in paragraph form.

7. Key findings from frequency distributions also can be presented more dramatically in bar charts and pie charts.

8. Examining cross-tabulations or associations among variables is usually the second step in quantitative data analysis. Cross-tabulation tables are more difficult to read than simple frequency distributions. These tables use percentage figures to describe possible associations among variables.

9. Stacked bar charts should be explored as an easy way to present cross-tabulation data.

10. Aside from interpreting trends based upon percentages, tests of statistical significance can be used as a way to determine in a more standardized manner if a relationship exists between two variables. The p level, or level of significance, tells you whether an association between two variables

is statistically significant. $P < .05$ is generally agreed to be the level beyond which a relationship is considered to be statistically significant or not.

11. Some common tests of statistical significances are chi-square for the association between two categorical variables, a t-test when you have one categorical variable with two categories and one continuous, interval level variable, and an F-test for one categorical variable with three or more categories and one continuous, interval level variable.

12. Qualitative data analysis can be especially helpful in presenting rich, descriptive data about program activities and outcomes.

13. Qualitative data analysis can be used to examine open-ended questions in a personal interview or questionnaire. The answers to the open-ended question should be transferred from the questionnaire to one large sheet of paper along with the respondents I.D. number. This makes its easier to examine trends in the responses.

14. In studies where qualitative data analysis is the major method of data analysis for process notes of direct observation, case records, and so on the following procedures of analysis should be followed. The analysis begins by reading all the descriptive data. Descriptive categories should be created. Some of these categories should be based upon program issues you decided to examine in your research plan, and other new categories will be created based ed upon the data you find. Finally, your descriptive data should be organized under the major categories of response, using the rich, descriptive quotes and passages to make your points.

EXERCISES FOR THIS CHAPTER

1. Think about implementing a study for a program you are acquainted with. Select a method of data collection from the previous chapter. What kinds of problems do you think you might experience as you collected the data for this evaluation?

2. Take a facesheet that records basic information on the clients or people in your agency or program. Take some real data or assume that you have data on 50 clients for the information on the sheet. Construct five tables of frequency distributions based upon the real data or the data you created for these 50 clients and discuss what you found in paragraph form. Present one bar chart and one pie chart for one of the descriptive characteristics you examined.

3. Take two questions from a questionnaire you constructed in the previous chapter or take two pieces of information on a client facesheet that you are familiar with. Specify two questions or pieces of information that you would like to cross-tabulate. Construct a cross-tabulation table and make up data you might find when you cross-tabulated the two pieces of informa-

tion. Compute column percentages and describe what you found. (For the truly brave.) Compute a chi-square based upon the data in your table.

4. Observe a program you know about in operation. Write two to three pages of notes based on your observations. Analyze these notes by describing some of the programming issues you uncovered.

REFERENCES

Craft, L. (1985) *Statistics and data analysis for social workers* (Itasca, IL: F.E. Peacock).

Morrison, D.E., & Henkel, R.E. (Ed.). (1970). *The significance tests controversy: A reader.* New York: Aldine de Gruyter.

Patton, M. Q. (1980). *Qualitative evaluation methods.* Newbury Park, CA: Sage Publications.

Scriven M. (1967). The methodology of evaluation. In R. Tyler, R.M. Gagne, & M. Scriven (Eds.). *Perspectives of curriculum evaluation.* (pp. 39–83). Chicago: Rand McNally.

Smith, M. J., Caro, F.G., & McKaig, K. (1987). *Caring for the developmentally disabled child at home: The experiences of low-income families.* New York: Community Service Society.

Tufte, E.R. (1983). *The visual display of quantitative information.* Chesire, C.T.

Weinbach, R.W., & Grinell, R.M. (1987). *Statistics for social workers.* New York: Longman. See especially, "Cross-tabluation," pp. 111-135 and "Comparison of Averages," pp. 158-176.

Williamson, J.B., Karp, D.A., Dalphin, J.R., & Gray, P.S. (1982). *The research craft: An introduction to social research methods* (2nd ed., pp. 203–208). Boston: Little, Brown & Co.

7

The Sixth Step: Reporting the Results of Program Evaluation

The final step in program evaluation comes after you have collected and analyzed all your data. First, you need to write a summary of major findings. Then, you need to make recommendations in terms of the program and its present and future directions. Finally, you need to put everything together in one final report from the first step of evaluation to the last step, from a description of the program through the summary and recommendations section.

FEEDBACK OF RESULTS

Probably *the* most important reason to do program evaluation is to *feed the results back for better, reality-based program planning*. In the last step of program evaluation, an all-out effort needs to be made so that relevant findings can affect the program itself. You do this through written and oral communication.

The most traditional method of communicating your results is through a written report. Minimally, you need to write a report that summarizes your findings and develops implications and recommendations. More properly, a comprehensive report needs to be written describing the program, the plan for evaluation, and the implementation of that plan through the data collection and data analysis. Reid described the major purpose of such a research report:

> The major purpose of a research report is to communicate to others the knowledge that has been derived from a particular study. To achieve this purpose, the

author customarily provides a rationale for conducting the study (in program evaluation, you describe the program and the need for evaluating it) and states the research problem (in program evaluation, what the goals were and whether the program is achieving its goals). The author then lays out the design and methods for the study and presents the findings and conclusions that the author has drawn from the study (including recommendations about the program). (1988 p. 447.)

Documenting the evaluation study in a written report is critical, but the researcher should not neglect oral presentation. You need to talk to people about your findings in an effort at understanding what they might mean in terms of the program. As a researcher engaged in the practice of program evaluation, you have discussed the program and the evaluation in the planning stages of the study. Now you should engage in formal and informal presentations and discussions with adminstrators, staff, funding sources, and consumer and community groups about what you found. This is especially helpful in moving from your findings in the data to recommendations. The more the institution is involved in helping form the recommendations, the more likely some planning action will be taken with the program.

THE CONSUMERS OF EVALUATIVE RESEARCH

Communicating the results of evaluative research can be a challenge because there is such a variety of possible audiences to reach. Before writing the report, the researcher needs to ask: "Who is the consumer of this evaluation?" The possibilities seem endless—the funding sources (federal, state or local governments, private foundations), the board of the agency where the program is located, the key executives in the organization, administrative staff, supervisors and middle-management personnel, direct-service workers, the consumers or clients of the service, the families of the clients, local community groups representing the clients or consumers of the service, and interested community groups and organizations.

Usually, the researcher communicates with those who have more power and administrative responsibility. The consumers of research are usually thought of as funding sources, boards, and administrative staff. Often, these are the people who authorized the evaluation in the first place and are paying the evaluator's salary. The researcher would certainly be unprofessional if he of she did not report back to those in charge.

In addition to reporting to these parties, however, the researcher needs to communicate with those lower down in the pecking order of the institution or agency. Reports of the evaluative findings should be shared with direct service staff. These are the people who do the work, who may have helped provide data for the study by being interviewed or helped you obtain access to clients to be interviewed. The clients or consumers who are receiving service have perhaps the largest stake in the program. Frequently, too there are community groups who represent the consumer and have an interest in the service being provided in their community.

The researcher should not be content to report to the usual people who affect programming decisions. In the first chapter, we suggested that interviewing clients in a research study *can* be a method of empowering them and seeing that their experiences with the program are reflected within the agency. Discussing the findings with the consumers of service or groups who represent clients or consumers can be a further way of empowering them within the agency or institution.

To achieve this goal of reaching all audiences, the research results need to be written and communicated in clear, non-technical language. The researcher needs to write the report so that people who are not trained in research methods, the average person, can read or understand what the study found.

> The cleaner and more simple the report, the more likely it is to be read and followed. The beginning researcher will do well to write short, clean sentences. Avoid long clauses that will lose the reader. Two short, clear sentences are preferable to one long, foggy one. . . . (Atherton & Klemmack, 1982, p. 503)

THE SOCIO-POLITICAL CONTEXT

Listing all the possible consumers of evaluative results shows that, like it or not, the researcher is deeply involved in the socio-political process of the organization. The researcher needs the ability to *assess and diagnose* this context in presenting findings and in arriving at recommendations. This is a critical practice activity in program evaluation. The researcher needs to assess the orientation of those involved at all levels if some action is desired as a result of the study. The researcher needs to determine how much movement is possible from each of the parties involved in using the study in an ongoing planning process. The importance of this political climate is clearly a factor that distinguishes program evaluation from research that is not conducted in an organizational setting.

The researcher needs to be an excellent politician. As with any political process, this involves the art of *negotiation and compromise.* You need to assess your audience and judge how much change is possible given the political climate. This process should involve compromises, not a total compromising of your findings and recommendations.

In theory, there should be open discussion of the findings and open debates which lead to better program planning. This can be a very creative and useful process, and an important outcome of evaluative research. This discussion and debate can actually be a section of the final report in the recommendations section and can lead to a more productive recommendations section. If there are irreconcilable differences between the researcher and the administrator, practice staff, or others, an *alternative view* section of the final report may need to be included. This section could include the debate among the key figures in program evaluation.

In practice, it takes extra resources to present and discuss findings with all those who are involved. Moreover, telling some people that they could do things better is sometimes interpreted by them to mean they were doing things wrong. In fact, those who need to change the most are usually the most defensive about the results of evaluative research. Reporting evaluative findings can induce conflicts between the researcher and *any* of the other parties involved. This can include the whole agency, funding sources, administrative staff, direct service staff, and client or consumer groups. These conflicts can take place over the findings, the recommendations, even over how the program is described. Each party has a personal and/or professional investment in how the program is planned, administered, and how it operates. All social institutions have a stake in not letting bad publicity surface. Sometimes it seems as though administrators would like to portray *all* programs they run as completely successful.

One example of a conflict between a researcher and practice staff can be shown in a memo I received from the director of a program and the practice staff of the program. Much of the conflict centered around the different perceptions of practice and research staff about the interventive methods that were provided. However, the conflict spilled over into all aspects of the evaluation.

> It is most regrettable to note that the presentation of the project experience is fraught with omissions, inaccurate information and distortions, since this poineering program has a great deal to offer. . . . The staff and I feel an ethical and professional obligation to comment on these critical factors since a gross injustice to the program, the clients, the staff and the agency will be committed. . . . Please note that we are not evaluating or "reviewing" the manuscript, but rather bringing your attention to matters of public record. . . . We will present as objective an account as possible. We cannot emphasize enough the urgency for an *honest* report of this program. . . .

This program director felt that facts were distorted and the researcher was dishonest. Calling for the need for an "honest" reporting and an "objective" account obviously indicate the high level of disagreement that was present between the researchers and the program staff. This is an example of the level of conflict that can occur between the researcher and others in the organization. The fact that often there may be only one or two researchers in the whole organization or that the researcher may be only a consultant or temporary employee of the organization makes the researcher's position even more difficult. In the real world, the researcher is involved in the *politics* of evaluation.

Another example of a conflict, this time a conflict between the researcher and a client group, comes from the single parent camp program which was mentioned in chapter one. The program, a two-week camp experience for single parents and their children, was admittedly poorly planned and implemented. The evaluative report reflected this. Discussion groups never materialized, which were to give single parents an orientation to living as a single parent and provide a self-help orientation for coping with the single-parent lifestyle. Administrators from the agency wanted to discontinue the camp program the next year because the results were so poor.

In discussing the evaluation report with the single parents who had gone to the camp, however, another perspective emerged. The parents were eager to go to camp again because it provided them with a break from their routine and they could not afford to take their children to camp without this program. The parents were greatly upset that the evaluation report portrayed the camp experience so negatively. Although the program part of the camp experience had been a disaster, they valued going to camp with their children. The client group attacked the evaluation report as a mechanism which kept them from going to camp. While from the agency point of view the program was a programming disaster, from the client point of view, the program had merit. The final report did not reflect the client point of view as much as it should have.

HOW TO WRITE THE RESEARCH REPORT

When you have arrived at this final stage of program evaluation, you should already have written at least a draft of your data analysis. You should have presented key data related to whether or not the major goals of the program have been achieved. You have presented frequency distributions on key variables. You have assessed relationships between the achievement of major goals and the characteristics of clients and the kinds of services with which they were provided through crosstabulation and other data analytic procedures. You have reported all your findings in narrative, paragraph and table form.

SUMMARY OF FINDINGS

Now, keeping the consumers of evaluative research in mind, you need to *summarize* your major findings from the study. Although you have already presented your findings in the data analysis, it is important to *restate* the major findings. The reader needs to be reacquainted with the major findings which were presented before with *all* the findings. The reader often forgets some of the findings from the data analysis section. Also, you want to single out the *major* findings so they can be kept separate from the recommendations and implications section. The findings are based directly on your data and the principles of data analysis as presented in the last chapter. There is less room for compromise in your data analysis, whereas, in recommendations for the program there is more room for interpretation and compromise. Reid cites the need to keep the findings separate from the recommendations and the author's use of the findings:

> The distinction between what has been found and the author's use of the findings must always be clear. If this distinction is not maintained, and if the findings and the means of obtaining them are distorted to advance the author's point of view, the purpose of the report will be badly subverted. (1988, p. 447)

Findings are usually tentative because we are usually not talking about cause-and-effect knowledge. You may not have conducted an experimental study in which you try to tease out intervening and confounding factors to determine what level of intervention caused what level of goal achievement.

On the other hand, you do not need to have an experimental design to state some clear findings. We need to be creative in relation to findings. One goal of social science research is descriptive. The findings can help us achieve better *descriptions* of the program, the logic with which the program operates, or the practice methodology. All are great benefits of program evaluation. Descriptive data, such as key descriptions of the program or program outcomes from the consumers or workers point of view or key quotes, are perfectly acceptable to have in your summary of findings.

Often descriptive research may be followed by another evaluative study that advances the level of methodology. For example, in the employee assistance program, the first study was a client follow-up study in which you asked clients their opinion of service. You may have found that many people thought they were feeling better about themselves because of the service. In the next evaluation, you might change the focus from an *ex post facto* study to a pre–post study in which you track changes in self esteem, marital relations, or other psychosocial measures for which change is sought.

An example of how the summary of findings might read is presented from the study of home care for families with developmentally disabled children, which was presented in the last chapter.

> In-home services are highly effective in serving their immediate purpose. Workers make the contribution expected of them. They provide direct care and many do it in ways that elicit a favorable response from the children. Workers relieve parents also by performing other household tasks. It is possible to find workers who perform well with these difficult assignments. For parents, in-home help provides a welcome opportunity to seek jobs, complete their education, catch up on household chores, spend times with other children, and sometimes simply rest. (Smith, Caro, & McKaig, 1987.)

Interpretation of Findings, Implications, and Recommendations

After the summary of findings, you need to draw some implications from your study and make some recommendations which come from your study findings. This means discussing what the evaluation means in terms of programs of this type, practice interventions, social problems, social policy, and so on. You need to discuss your findings in relation to all of the areas of the program described earlier in your research plan. You should start out logically and pragmatically in terms of immediate problems facing this immediate program, and gradually increase the implications to a local, national, or even world vision of why we should or should not have programs such as this one and what it means.

Any specific recommendations you make should be thought through in terms of implementation. People charged to make changes are more likely to respond positively if the logical consequences of those recommendations are presented. An example of recommendation and implications reported in the home care study for families raising developmentally disabled children is presented here as an example. This evaluative report raised some issues about the administration of home care services based on certain negative incidents of home care service found in this study and this led to some major recommendations.

> At the time the interviews were conducted, families were generally satisfied with their help. Many, however, had gone through a number of workers before they settled on one who was satisfactory. The descriptions of the care needs of the families make it clear that workers are needed who are not only responsible but who have some knowledge of the specific needs of

these children and who know how to interact with them in a caring way. The assignment of an untrained workers means that parents often have to spend a great deal of time training the worker. If the worker is not skilled and responsible, the worker makes little, if any, contribution. The experiences of parents point to a need for better screening, training, and supervision of these workers. (Smith, Caro, & McKaig, 1987.)

The Complete Evaluative Report

After writing a summary of findings and conclusions and implications, you rewrite earlier parts of what was your research plan but now becomes your final report. There are no surprises here, in fact, the outline of your final report is similar to the outline of the evaluative process in this book.

1. Program Description
2. The Program Goals and Objectives
3. The Research Plan or Design
    The Research Design
    Data Collection Procedures
    The Research Instrument
    Sampling Plan
4. The Analysis of Data
5. Summary of Findings
6. Implications and Recommendations

The one addition to this outline may be what is called an "executive summary" in the beginning of the report. This summary is an overview of the evaluative problem, the program that was evaluated, the methods of evaluation, and, most importantly, a summary of the findings and recommendations. This allows the person reading the report, whether it be an executive or a person served by the program, to read the highlights of the report in anywhere from three to ten pages.

Other than the summary and overview section, the above outline provides the basic framework of how to present the report. The headings and subheadings can be made more interesting and substantive. For example, "The Program Description" can be changed to "Description of the Employee Assistance Program" or "Implications and Recommendations" can be presented as "Future Directions for the Employee Assistance Program."

The remaining sections are written by reviewing your original study plan. You need to describe the program and things you discovered about the program while you were planning the study. You describe the program clientele and program methods, and the organizational context of the program. You describe all the goals of the program and single out those goals you have chosen for study. You restate what the study plan was and the methods of data collection and sampling. (Very specific or technical aspects of the plan such as the actual questionniare or mechanics of the sampling process should be placed in an appendix to the report.) At the end of the section on the research plan, you need to say how the study was implemented and what changes were made as the study was implemented and the data was collected.

The analysis of data, summary of findings, and recommendations sections that have been written in the process of conducting the evaluation can now be integrated into the one final report. The process is now complete. Hopefully, many of the recommendations will be acted on and the organization will continue to evaluate programs in the hopes of improving them.

SUMMARY OF KEY IDEAS IN THIS CHAPTER

1. Probably the most important reason to conduct program evaluation is to feedback the results into a reality-based program planning process.

2. Findings and recommendations should be reported to the consumers of research in both oral and written form and in clear and simple language.

3. The traditional consumers of evaluative research are funding sources, boards of directors, executives, and administrators. Special efforts are needed to communicate with direct service staff, clients and consumers, and community organizations that represent client and consumer groups.

4. In making recommendations for the program, the researcher needs to diagnose the political climate of the organization. A certain amount of conflict is inevitable in making recommendations about the program.

5. A complete report of the evaluative study includes reporting on all the different stages of program evaluation, starting from describing the program to summarizing the findings and recommendations.

EXERCISES FOR THIS CHAPTER

1. Choose a program you are acquainted with. Although you did not evaluate the program, what are your recommendations on how a program administrator could improve the program. Consider this as an exercise in how to write a recommendation and implications section in the evaluative report.

2. Discuss a number of ways in which you might overcome possible conflict with administrators and practice staff in reporting the results of evaluation research and in suggesting changes in the program.

REFERENCES

Atherton, R., & Klemmack, D.L. (1982). *Research methods in social work.* Lexington, MA: D.C. Heath & Co.

Reid, W.J. (1988). Research reports and publication procedures. In R.M. Grinnell (ed.), *Social work research and evaluation* (pp. 446–464). Itasca, IL: F.E. Peacock.

Smith, M.J., Caro, F., & McKaig, K. (1987). *Caring for the developmentally disabled child at home: The experiences of low-income families.* New York: The Community Service Society.

Appendix A:
Example of the Evaluation
Research Plan Needed for a
Proposal for a Training Contract

Often social service agencies, schools, hospitals, or other institutional settings apply for funding to train staff in their institutions or in agencies they work with to help improve the delivery of services. The funding body may be a federal, state or local government agency or a private foundation. For example, you may wish to obtain outside funds to train your staff in helping persons with AIDS, to train some of your staff to work with the homeless, or to train staff to prepare clients for discharge or service termination at your hospital, school, or social service agency.

In writing a proposal for funding, you would need to prepare a plan for the training, a curriculum, a plan for how the training would take place, and the training methodology. You would also need to develop a plan for evaluation of the training program proposal. This is a clear, concrete example of how you need to know at least the basics of program evaluation in your role as a professional.

The funding source for whom you are developing the proposal would most likely require that you outline your posposal in the following way. First, they would want to see the plan for training. Second, they would require that you specify how you would evaluate the training.

THE TRAINING PROGRAM PROPOSAL

1. The Plan for the Training

A. *The Purpose of the Training.* Specify the need for the training. What is the overall purpose of the training and why is it needed at this time in your agency or community? How many sessions will be conducted over what period of time? Who will conduct the training and what qualifications do they have to conduct such training?

List the objectives for each of the training sessions to be conducted. List some of the objectives in behavioral terms. Which new skills, knowledge or attitudes will be changed by the end of the training? How will you demonstrate such change.

B. *Major Curriculum Areas and Major Concepts Involved in the Training.* Provide a description of the curriculum. Which areas will be covered and in which sequence will they be taught? Describe the major theories and concepts which will be presented and describe why they are important.

C. *Major Training Methods and Activities.* Describe the overall orientation to the training in terms of teaching approach. Describe the specific methodologies employed in each session. Will you use lecture/disscussion, role-playing, small task-oriented groups, films, videos? How much time will each type of teaching methodology be used? Present the types of questions that will be utilized to promote group discussions. Present an outline of the methodologies used in each session. Provide examples of training materials that will be given directly to the participants.

2. The Plan for Evaluating the Training Program

The following is a list of the *minimum* evaluation requirements that must be described before your proposal will be considered for funding. The methodologies of program evaluation should be used to comprehensively and objectively assess the effectiveness of the training. At the conclusion of the training program, you must be able to specify whether the training objectives were met. In specifying an evaluation method, you must cite the literature on program evaluation to indicate the strengths and the limitations of the particular type of research plan you are using.

The plan for evaluating the training *must* include the following elements. First, attempts must be made to interview or handout questionnaires to *every* training participant, whether they completed the full training program or not. Second, the evaluation must measure the effect of the training in terms of increased knowledge, increased professional skills, and/or a change in attitude or approach to some population, client group or practice methodology. Third, the evaluation should include some type of follow up plan to assess the value of the training in terms of better functioning on the job, better attitude toward the work, or indications that the training actually made a difference in job performance.

The following should be part of your evaluation plan:

A. An *ex post facto* Interview or Questionnaire. This instrument must be given to *all* participants.

B. *A pre–post design.* This instrument establishes plausible explanations for *changes* in knowledge, attitudes, skills, and behavior as a result of the training.

C. *A two-month follow-up.* The follow-up period establishes the impact of the training, including the sampling plan and plans for data collection. Discuss what obstacles will be overcome to initiate the two-month follow-up.

D. *Photocopies.* Copies of all the questionnaires, interviews and other evaluation data collection instruments must be included with your proposal.

E. *The Evaluation Plan.* Your final plan must include a description of how initial evaluation results will be used to change the training and improve the training curriculum and training methodologies over the life of the training program.

F. *The Evaluation Plan.* The plan of evaluation should include an outline for quarterly reports to be submitted for each fiscal quarter throughout the period of funding. The complete plan for evaluating the training program will be reviewed closely by our subcommittee on program evaluation.

Appendix B: University Employee Assistance Program Service Form for Input to Management Information System

---

Client Information

1. Date of First Contact __ / __ / __
   Month Day Year

2. Type of Contact ____ (1) in-person ____ (2) telephone

3. Is the client: (check one)

   ____ (1) an employee

   ____ (2) an employee's spouse

   ____ (3) an employee's child

   ____ (4) another relative

   ____ (5) other list _____

4. Age ____

5. Gender: ____ (1) male ____ (2) female

6. Marital status

   ____ (1) married

   ____ (2) single

   ____ (3) divorced/separated

   ____ (4) widowed

7. Race:

       ____ (1) White, non-Hispanic

       ____ (2) Black, non-Hispanic

       ____ (3) White, Hispanic

       ____ (4) Asian

       ____ (5) Other (list) _____

8. Employee's Job Classification

       ____ (1) Administrative, Higher Education Officer

       ____ (2) Faculty

       ____ (3) Secretarial/Clerical

       ____ (4) Custodial/Maintenance

       ____ (5) Other list _____

9. Employee is: ____ (1) a supervisor   ____ (2) non-supervisor

10. Employment status: ____ (1) full time   ____ (2) part time

11. Number of years employed at the University: ____

CONTACT INFORMATION

12. Primary Referral Source: (check one)

       ____ (1) self

       ____ (2) other employee

       ____ (3) supervisor

       ____ (4) union

       ____ (5) family

       ____ (6) other list _____

13. Reason for contact: (check one)

       ____ (1) information and/or referral

       ____ (2) problem assessment and service

       ____ (3) consultation to supervisor or management

       ____ (4) other _____

14.   Service needs: (check all that apply)

      ____ (1) Financial

      ____ (2) Legal/Consumer

      ____ (3) Housing

      ____ (4) Social Service

      ____ (5) Personal Adjustment

      ____ (6) Mental Illness

      ____ (7) Job Related Stress

      ____ (8) Alcohol Abuse

      ____ (9) Substance Abuse

      ____ (10) Interpersonal

      ____ (11) Couple/Family

      ____ (12) Physical Health

      ____ (13) Physical/Sexual Abuse

      ____ (14) Alcohol Abuse in Family/Significant Other

      ____ (15) Substance Abuse in Family/Significant Other

      ____ (16) Other: _____

                _____

15.   Number of *Primary* Problem from above list: _____

16.   Services to be provided at the Employee Assistance Program:

    (check all that apply)

      ____ (1) Information

      ____ (2) Individual

      ____ (3) Couple/Family

      ____ (4) Group

      ____ (5) Advocacy

17.   Referrals Made to Other Agencies:

      (check all that apply)

      _____   (1) Financial

      _____   (2) Legal

      _____   (3) Social Service

      _____   (4) Educational

      _____   (5) Housing

      _____   (6) Health Care

      _____   (7) Mental Health

      _____   (8) Family

      _____   (9) In-Patient

      _____ (10) Self-help

      _____ (11) Union

      _____ (12) Other list _____

Appendix C: University Employee Assistance Program Client Satisfaction Questionnaire

---

The Employee Assistance Program would like to know if we have served you well. Please take 5 minutes to tell us about your experience with the service by answering following questions.

Note that this information is completely confidential. Do not put your name on this questionnaire. Notice too that we did not ask you any identifying information such as the department where you work, your position at the University or any information such as age, marital status, etc.

When you have completed the questionnaire, simply place it in the enclosed stamped envelope and put it in a mailbox.

Your candid responses to the following questions will help us improve services to you and to your fellow employees at the University.

Thank you.

1. Which of the following best describe the kind of situation or problem for which you sought help at the Employee Assistance Program? (Check as many as apply.)

_____ trouble getting along with a spouse or someone with whom you share a close personal relationship

_____ trouble with a child in your family

_____ trouble getting along with another family member, relative, or friend

_____ stress from a change in living circumstances

_____ trouble carrying out responsibilities at home

_____ trouble carrying out responsibilities at work

_____ physical or health problems

_____ financial problems

_____ trouble getting along with someone at work (e.g., co-worker, or supervisor)

_____ general irritability at work

_____ trouble dealing with feelings or emotions

_____ drinking or drug problems

_____ other; please describe: _____

2. Was the problem that brought you to the Employee Assistance Program negatively affecting your experience at work in any of the following ways)? (Check all that apply.)

A. less satisfaction from my job   __ Yes __ No __ Somewhat

B. reduced ability to concentrate at work   __ Yes __ No __ Somewhat

C. more absences or lateness   __ Yes __ No __ Somewhat

D. not doing my work as well as I usually do __ Yes __ No __ Somewhat

E. trouble getting along with others at work __ Yes __ No __ Somewhat

3. Did anyone suggest that you go to the Employee Assistance Program?

_____ No

_____ Yes, a co-worker

_____ Yes, my supervisor

_____ Yes, someone else, e.g. family member, personal friend, etc., please list

their relationship to you (not their actual name)

_____

4. In your opinion, did the Employee Assistance Program respond to your particular problem quickly?

_____ Yes

_____ No

_____ Somewhat

If no please explain: _____

_____

6. What would you say the EAP staff person did for you?

7. How frequently did you usually meet with the EAP staff person?

____ once a week

____ about every other week

____ about once a month

____ less frequently than once month

8. Were you satisfied with how often the EAP staff person met with you?

____ Yes

____ No, would have like less frequent contacts

____ No, would have liked more frequent contacts

9. How helpful would you say the EAP staff were to you?

____ extremely helpful

____ somewhat helpful

____ not particularly helpful

10. Specifically, what did the EAP staff person do for you that was helpful or not helpful?

11. How do you feel your situation or problem has changed since you first contacted the EAP?

____ become much better

____ become a little better

____ not much change

____ become a little worse

____ become much worse

Why do you say this? _____

_____

12. In general, what do you think of the service that you received from the Employee Assistance Program?

_____ very satisfied

_____ satisfied

_____ neither satisfied nor dissatisfied

_____ dissatisfied

_____ very dissatisfied

13. Did the Employee Assistance Program make you feel better about yourself in any way?

_____ Yes   _____ No _____ Somewhat

14. Did the Employee Assistance Program make a difference in your personal life?

_____ Yes   _____ No _____ Somewhat

15. Did the Employee Assistance Program make a difference in your work on the job?

_____ Yes   _____ No _____ Somewhat

16. If you encountered a problem in the future, would you consider returning to the Employee Assistance Program?

_____ Yes   _____ No _____ Not Sure

17. If a friend asked, would you recommend the Employee Assistance Program?

_____ Yes   _____ No _____ Not Sure

In the space below, please make any comments about the service that was provided to you by the Employee Assistance Program or make any suggestions you may have about new ways we might help you or others at the University.

Thank You. We appreciate your help. Now simply place the questionnaire in the stamped envelope and mail it back to us.

Author Index

Atherton, R., 132

Babbie, E., 27
Backstrom, C. H., 102
Borgatta, E., 36
Bradshaw, J., 59

Caro, F. G., 69,123,136,137–138
Craft, J., 121

Dalphin, J. R., 122

Etzioni, A., 33

Frankfather, D. L., 61
Freeman, H. E., 11,21,30,49

Gray, P. S., 122
Grinnell, R. M., 121

Henkel, R. E., 118
Hursh, G. D., 102

Jayaratne, S., 53
Jones, W., 36

Karp, D. A., 122
Kent, M. L., 22
Kiresuk, T. J., 53
Klemmack, D. L., 132

Kogan, L. S., 51

Levy, R., 53
Lewis, H., 19

McKaig, K., 123,136,137–138
Meyer, H., 36
Morrison, D. E., 188

Patton, M. Q., 21,56
Polansky, N. A., 22

Reid, W. J., 36,130–131,135
Rosenberg, M., 57
Rossi, P. H., 11,21,30,49
Ryan, W., 25

Scriven, M., 52,107
Sherman, R. E., 53
Shyne, A. W., 36,51
Smith, M. J., 69,123,136,137,138
Smith, M. L., 7
Suchman, E. A., 34,40,50

Tripodi, T., 11,71
Tufte, E. R., 110

Weinbach, R. W., 121
Weiss, C. H., 11,21,28,56
Williamson, J. B., 122

Subject Index

Ex post facto survey design; *see*
    Surveys, Research design

Formative evaluation, 51–52, 107

Goal-attainment scaling, 53
Goals; *see* Program goals

Knowledge-building about
    programming, 23–24

Management by objective, 50
Management information system,
    60–61
    example of a form, 143–146
Monitoring studies; *see* Program
    monitoring

Needs assessment studies, 19,37–41
    cautions about needs assessment
      studies, 40–41
    census data in, 39
    definition, 37
    survey in a needs assessment study,
      37–39
    survey of potential consumers, 39
    review of literature in, 39
N of 1 case study, 50

Observation; *see* Data collection
Observational studies; *see* Data
    collection
Objectives; *see* Program objectives
Operationalization, 47,62–63

Personal interviews; *see* Data collection
PERT model of program evaluation, 50
Politics of program evaluation, 20–21,
    132–134
Population, *see* Sampling, Target
    population
Pre–post studies; *see* Research design
Process evaluations, 20
Process objectives, 47
Process studies; *see* Program
    monitoring
Program attrition, 96,99
Program evaluation,
    applying techniques in practice, 7–9
    conflicts in reporting findings,
      133–134

consumers of, 131–132
definition, 15,15–21
field of research, 19–20
implementing the evaluation,
    105–106
politics of, 20–21
practice of, 17–19, 49
reporting results, 130–138
steps in, 12
summative–formative, 51
systems approach, 33–34
techniques of, 7–10
tender-hearted versus tough-minded
    approaches, 51
training programs and, 140–142
writing the evaluation report,
    134–138
Program goals,
    case example of goals in child
      welfare, 62–67
    as change in knowledge, attitude,
      skills and behavior, 54–56
    as dependent variables, 44–46
    importance of, 43
    long-term goals, 50–51
    multiple goals, 52
    operationalization of, 47
    practice goals, 52–53
    and program objectives, 46–47
    proximate goals, 50–52
    reliability of, 56–58
    short-term goals, 50–51
    typologies of goals, 50–56
    ultimate goals, 50–51
    unanticipated goals and
      consequences, 53–54
    validity of, 56, 58–59
Program monitoring studies, 59–62
    examples of, 60–61
    program operations, 60
Program objectives, *see* Program goals
Program outcomes, 6; *see also* Program
    goals
Programs; *see* Social programs
Proximate goals, *see* program goals

Questionnaire construction, 84–93
Questionnaires; *see* Data collection
Quasi-experimental design, *see*
    Experimental design